TARGET TERRORISM:
Providing Protective Services

RICHARD W. KOBETZ, D.P.A. and H.H.A. COOPER, LL.M.

Bureau of Operations
and Research
International Association
of Chiefs of Police

ELEVEN FIRSTFIELD ROAD, GAITHERSBURG, MARYLAND

Library of Congress Cataloging in Publication Data

Main entry under title:
Target Terrorism:
Providing Protective Services

ISBN-0-88269-050-7

Printed in the United States of America

To all the unsung heroes of public and private law enforcement who daily place their lives and reputations on the line.

Preface

This book is intended as a response to a felt need. It is the product of a singular kind of experience that merits some explanation of its own. The International Association of Chiefs of Police has been involved, since its founding in 1893, in various aspects of police education and training. It has consistently aimed for excellence in the various fields of endeavors it has entered, and the modern phenomenon of terrorism has called forth from the Association a systematic and thoughtful response. The various programs of professional training produced by the Association in recent years have sought to meet the turns and convolutions of this constantly changing phenomenon. The experience that has been gained by the small team of instructors engaged in undertaking the work of training for the Association has likewise changed and developed with the phenomenon of terrorism itself.

This book represents the fruits of that experience as they have been gathered at a particular point in time. While it is hoped that these are of a maturity and ripeness that would permit their useful consumption at this moment, it must be stressed that nothing in this book is to be taken as final or the last word on the subject. The process of evolution of terrorism and counterterrorism continues; and the staff of the International Association of Chiefs of Police, together with their consultants, are constantly engaged in studies to devise better methods of response to this ugly phenomenon. While the book is, therefore, of a provisional character, it does represent the experience gained to date and its reduction to a useful, instructional form. It is not a collection or distillation of existing training materials, but rather something quite different that has emerged or grown out of them, and out of the practical experience of trying to teach certain principles in a very special setting to a very special group of people. It is some of this teaching—and learning—experience that it is hoped this text will convey.

A central feature of the training in this area that is offered by the International Association of Chiefs of Police is that of the team concept. It may well be that some teams must have a leader, and they most certainly have personnel with some aptitudes that are not shared by other members of the team. Different members of the team have different functions, but it is always their team effort that produces the final satisfactory result. So it is with the present book, that although the writing of it has been, substantially, the burden of the authors, the text is intended to reflect the vast amount of consultation, long hours of discussion and argument, and a continual monitoring of others' experiences that have left their mark in the final product. In particular, it would be invidious not to mention prominently in this preface the interactions and contributions of other members of the team that have combined to shape and define this finished work. Special reference should be made to Eugene Ferrara, Irving Goldaber, David C. Hart, David G. Hubbard, William Penn, and S.D. Vestermark, Jr., all of whose good fellowship, excellent scholarship, and dedication to the tasks in hand have served to encourage and stimulate the authors in the analysis and interpretation of the difficult subjects treated herein.

No educational endeavor of this kind can hope for success without a host of administrative and other staff helpers whose work, while it does not figure so prominently in the technical aspects of the text, is nevertheless a vital support service without which the book itself would never see the light of day. Many hands have helped to make light work not only of the book itself but of the tremendous amount of educational work that has gone into the preparation and production of the International Association of Chiefs of Police seminars on Protective Services and Responses to Hostage Taking. It is hoped that those who have performed these unsung roles from time to time will feel gratified at seeing some of the results of their own labors in this printed form.

Richard W. Kobetz
H.H.A. Cooper

Table of Contents

	Page
Introduction	3
Targets of Terrorism	7
Tactics of Terrorism	16
Assassinations	24
Kidnapping	55
Hostage Taking	79
Bombing, Firesetting and Contamination	89
Extortion	112
Terrorist Profiles	118
Terrorism: When and Where	148
Reducing the Risk	160
Conclusion	175
Bibliography	179
Index	192

"Individual violence is now more often used than invasion or bombardment as a means of international coercion, and is proving more effective than public demonstrations and riots for exerting internal pressure. Guerrillas and terrorists have existed for centuries, but it is only in the last few years that they have become a substantial force in international affairs and internal politics which it is vitally important for the people of the world to understand."

Richard Clutterbuck[1]

Introduction

The term *security* means different things to different people. In one sense, security is an end in itself, while in another it is a way of attaining that end. Basically, all these notions involve the idea of making people and things safe from some kind of danger. Danger, in itself, is not necessarily a bad thing. While under some circumstances danger might serve as a necessary stimulus or excitement to human growth and endeavor,[2] the result of an overstimulus, where there is an *ever-present* danger of the willful destruction of life and property, is inhibiting and harmful to the proper development of human relationships. Such dangers constitute an adverse influence against which human beings need *protection.* The need to be *secure* in their persons and property in order to function as human beings and in order to function, effectively, as a community is basic and common to all. Security, therefore, in its most important meaning, is nothing more than the protection of individuals and the community from those dangers that would threaten their existence or proper functioning.

The deliberate creation of destructive danger engenders high levels of anxiety and fear. *Fear* is an intrusive emotion capable of penetrating the security that surrounds the human individual, alone or in society, so as to destroy the potential for a serene collective or individual existence. When *fear* is generated in sufficient proportions and directed for coercive purposes it becomes *terroristic* in nature. *Terrorism* is the application of this massive fear *by* human beings against other human beings for the purpose of destroying their relationships, their physical integrity, their property, and other interests.[3] Security is not only safety, but also freedom from fear. The security system that is necessary to safeguard the individual and the community from the interference and harm posed by this threat is the product of counter responses that are of a *protective* character. The protective services that furnish such security must be of the kind capable of offering a sustained and effective response to those forces seeking to destroy the individual in society by terroristic means. Such services require constant updating, for the opponent is always seeking new ways of breaking through the security system designed to keep him out.

Security, in the sense in which the term is used here, is the invisible barrier against certain dangers provided by an effective system of protective services. Protective services comprise the procedures and techniques, as well as the physical and psychological means, whereby the safety of the individual and the community, as well as their respective interests, is assured.

The human individual in modern society is threatened by a multitude of dangers, some of his own making, some natural or environmental, and some deliberately aimed at him by others. Hazards, natural disasters, even the products of his own carelessness, threaten his security on a continuing basis. Security against the misfortunes that would otherwise threaten him is assured by a variety of devices, many of which have a character analogous to the kind of protective services that form the subject of the present instruction.[4] Here, however, the threat to the security of the individual, and to the community of which he forms part, is defined as a comparatively narrow one, namely that posed by violent, subversive or clandestine groups opposed to the monopoly on the use of force vested in the modern state. These groups are, for the present purposes, those having some political objective related directly or indirectly, to the overthrow of the state or society in its present form rather than antisocial groups having a purely criminal purpose and which are simply engaged in the breaking of law rather than in seeking destruction of the very framework of law through a violent, ideological opposition to it. Criminal enterprises of other kinds certainly pose a very severe threat to the security of the individual and to the community, but they do not form the subject of the present text in so far as the protective measures designed to combat terrorism and quasi-terrorism are of incidental value in these cases also. Thus, in some countries—Italy for example—methods, such as kidnapping, employed by terrorists are virtually indistinguishable from those employed by common criminals.[5] Because the motivation and objectives differ quite radically, however, responses that are of value in the one case may be quite useless in the other. The protective services, with which this text is concerned, have as their objective the safeguarding of the individual and the community against enterprises which, though criminal in character and execution, are also of a political or ideological character implying a *total rejection* of the established legal, political, social or economic systems so as to require their overthrow in the power struggle. This fact gives the security aspects in question their peculiar character, and the responses to the hazards posed by this behavior are of an order somewhat different from those required in the fight against common crime. This must be well understood by anyone engaged in a professional study of protective services.

The objective of those engaged in this type of terrorist behavior is thus nothing less than the destruction of the established system of law and order and the substitution of a radically different power structure that would favor their cause. Although it manifests itself in the form of violent action, this type of threat is of a covert rather than an open character and for this reason the *clandestine nature* of this conduct has been emphasized here.[6] It will be appreciated that the harmful, destructive behavior against which protection is necessary will be made manifest only after a period of clandestine planning and preparation, and this has to be continually emphasized in the protective aspects. The watchword of these readings is that *prevention is better than cure.* Protection implies full knowledge of what might occur and a consistent pattern of activity designed to avert harm rather than one capable only of producing a reactive response to the harm intended by the actor. *Foresight* and *preparation* are, therefore, erected as a bulwark against the *surprise* and *initiative* of those who would harm the protected individual and the community in this way. *Full security comes from leaving nothing undone.*[7]

It is thus evident that a restricted notion of security is implied by the present system of instruction. No blanket, all-embracing system of protective services is realistic. It is concerned with the security of particular individuals and interests against the hazards posed by particular threats. It is thus pertinent to inquire *who* is the subject of the protective services envisaged, and *what* is the threat against which such protection has been designed?

NOTES

1. *Guerillas and Terrorists* (London: Faber and Faber, 1977), p. 13.
2. There are interesting parallels in the animal world. "Occasionally insects become so intolerable that the entire head can be seen shaking and twitching and changing direction to escape. All this misery is for the good of the species, of course, or else it might overbreed, overbrowse and starve." Robert Campbell, "The Interaction of Two Great Rivers Help Sustain the Earth's Vital Biosphere," *Smithsonian,* September, 1977, p. 47.
3. On this, see H.H.A. Cooper, "The Terrorist and the Victim," *Victimology,* Vol. 1, No. 2, June, 1976.

4. The notion of security is universal. It is the character of the dangers themselves, their source and direction that impress themselves in distinctive fashion on the measures of protection taken. The medical model is well worth comparison in this regard.
5. Of the kidnapping in Paris of the Belgian Baron Empain, it is said: "At first, authorities believed both attacks were 'German-style' kidnappings—planned for political reasons by terrorists like West Germany's Baader-Meinhof Gang, which seized and then murdered German industrialist Hanns-Martin Schleyer last year. But the evidence suggested that Empain, at least, was a victim of kidnapping 'Italian style'—purely for profit." *Newsweek,* 6, 1978, p. 49.
6. This is well understood by terrorist movements. It was said in Tsarist Russia: "When three men gather to discuss revolution, two are secret policemen and one is a fool."
7. It has been well said that: "Not to plan rationally for a stressful situation is to court self-destruction." Samuel Z. Klausner, "Empirical Analysis of Stress-Seekers," *Why Man Takes Chances* (New York: Anchor Books, 1968), p. 143.

Targets of Terrorism

"The concept of victim appears among the most ancient ones of humanity. Inextricably connected with the idea and practice of sacrifice, the notion of victim belongs to all cultures."

Emilio C. Viano[1]

Protection of Whom?

In one sense, protective services are designed to ensure the security of *any* person or interests, tangible or intangible, against which a threat is posed by clandestine activity. The extent of the threat, its nature and intensity, is determined by a study of the target population itself. For example, a threat might be posed specifically against some particular individual by reason of his or her inherent importance in the system or community of which they form a part. A public figure associated with some institution or enterprise in a direct and personal fashion might constitute a high-risk, symbolic target.[2] An individual having some particular skill or unique qualities might be a security risk because of his value to those he serves.[3] On the other hand, the risk may be of a more diffuse nature and directed at unspecified or, for the moment, unidentified individuals within the community either singly or as a group.[4] Their personal security may be threatened, indiscriminately, by those seeking simply to use them as an example to intimidate others. For these reasons, *all* may be said to be in need of protection in varying degrees, but the threat to some persons will clearly be more substantial and evident than to others. The nature and quality of the protection to be afforded the individual and the community are determined by an appropriate assessment of the type and intensity of the risk to which they are each exposed. It may be said, broadly, that some persons are exposed to a risk against which protection must be given on account of *what* they do. Protection must be oriented accordingly. Sometimes, the threat is directed against the whole community, in general, in a non-specific way.[5] Protective services designed to meet these kinds of threats must, therefore, have to reflect their general or special character. Just as it may be asked, who are likely to be victims of heart attacks, so, too, may the question be posed: Who is likely to be a victim of terrorism? The same *techniques* of threat analysis may be used in each case. Often, an entire community constitutes the client population for such a general query as that posed here, but it is evident that a more precise reply can only be given from an analysis of the situation as it exists at any particular place and time. Target figures may not always be precisely identifiable, but in any terroristic campaign, patterns of action develop so that groups or clusters of persons can be clearly seen as bearing a higher risk potential than others. Risk factors are variable from place to place and person to person. Persons who are safe in one place, may not be safe in another.[6] Time is also an important factor in risk assessment. Persons who might be safe at one point in time are clearly likely to be threatened at another. The danger may be transitory or relatively permanent and may fluctuate for a variety of causes. Protective systems must be responsive to the variations. While it may not be possible to predict with a high degree of accuracy all those who are subject to attack by terrorists, it is certainly possible to establish with a fair measure of certainty those who face a particular risk of harm from this source. From time to time, and place to place, terrorists' objectives and targets alter but it is always possible to determine, especially during the course of a period of intense activity, who is likely to present a peculiarly high risk of involvement and to structure a pattern of response designed to give a useful measure of protection to such individuals and the communities in which they find themselves. *The greatest danger to effective action is in ignoring the obvious risks.* That the individuals exposed to the risks might choose to overlook or minimize them is understandable and easily explainable on psychological grounds.[7] That those whose duty it is to protect them should fall into the same way of thinking is unforgivable.

In general, the protection of the community in a non-specific fashion will fall to the lot of the public law enforcement agencies. The protection of particular individuals and their interests from the special hazards that they may face will be primarily the responsibility of private security forces engaged for that purpose. The division of responsibilities is not, however, a hard and fast one. The two functions may, on occasion, overlap. Where a private individual is seen to be exposed to a particularly high threat of a known or specified kind, additional precautions on the part of the appropriate public law enforcement agencies may be necessary in that instance. Such is the case where an individual is the target of specific threats, or information is received that he or she is likely to be subject to some attack by terrorist groups. Certain individuals who hold sensitive positions, are in the public eye, or are engaged in controversial activities of some kind, are not infrequently exposed to particular threats of this sort requiring intervention by the public law enforcement agencies. The general, overall security of such individuals, is however, largely a private matter, and the preventive aspects of protective services are extremely important in their case. The real distinction between the public and private functions of protection lies in the transitory nature of one against the semi-permanent nature of the other. The services must, in the first place, be geared to minimize the risk. In the second place, they must be prepared to offer a rapid protective response should the apprehended harm materialize. Those concerned with the design and provision of protective services must be able to appreciate the nature of the type of harm threatened and correctly gauge the direction of the threat.

It is particularly important to recognize that the attack upon a chosen target individual may be oblique rather than direct. For example, if the terroristic threat of harm is designed to put pressure upon some individual to get him to do, or forbear to do, something contrary to his duty or desires, then it may be that an attack of some kind will be made not upon his person directly but upon members of his family or those assumed to enjoy some special relationship with him. The protection of such individuals is, thus, naturally related in the most direct way to the protection of those other persons with whom they are involved. Unless there is some pressing reason to the contrary, terrorists will attack lightly protected rather than heavily protected targets. The protection of the target individual can only be effectively secured by having a network of protection that extends to *all* his interests and covers *all* relationships that might be damaged by persons having inimical objectives.

The protection of *whom* is also intimately connected with the protection of *what*. Sometimes the true object of the attack is a material, though intangible, interest, such as a business or professional relationship, or a symbolic interest; and the human individuals involved are merely the means or channel through which the attack upon these interests is pressed home. If, for example, the real objective were to drive a particular business out of a certain area, then the object of attack would be the individuals conducting the business in that area.[8] This is what has happened in many Latin American countries where the kidnapping and assassination of American and other foreign businessmen has not been directed, necessarily, at the human individuals personally but rather at the notion of foreign business, the hated "imperialist capitalism" which those opposed to it are trying to eradicate.[9] In such cases, what must be protected are the business interests and the business relationships involved, but this necessarily requires protection of the human individuals engaged in their operation. Whatever the terrorist strategy, the overall objectives of protective services remain the same. It may however, be necessary, to devise different means for the protection of the individual from those means than would be necessary to protect the intangible and property interests involved. Difficulties may arise where there is a conflict of interest, and it is necessary for the protective services to be established with various priorities in mind. It is important, too, to determine how local law might affect those priorities and policy goals.

The protection of any particular individual or any particular interest cannot be dealt with in isolation. Security has its own system of inter- and intradependent relationships. The need for protection must be seen in the entire social context. There must, accordingly, be an integrated protective response if it is to be effective. The interdependency of human relations among individuals and the interrelation of their various interests must be thoroughly explored and understood, both in the abstract and the particular, if an effective scheme of protective responses is to be designed. An individual who represents an especially high risk may need particular protective measures in relation to his person and activities, for example, bodyguards, protective clothing, special security devices to make entry to his home or place of business more easily controllable, and a variety of other measures designed to give him a high degree of personal security. None of these steps will be effective, however, if the relationship that he enjoys with other people is ignored in the protective planning and if he is left vulnerable as a result of a collateral attack upon persons with whom he is intimately associated. Terroristic enterprises carry a message. They seek to impress.[10] The people at whom the message of fear is directed is not always the immediate victim.[11]

Good security requires, indispensably, the fullest cooperation of the person whose interests are to be protected. Many persons tend, consciously or unconsciously, to contribute to their own victimization. This is most frequently done by undervaluing the effectiveness of the personnel and procedures established to that end. The individual thus contributes in the most intense and effective way to the destruction of his own security. Some individuals seem deliberately to court danger, eluding their bodyguards, taking unplanned detours, dashing impetuously into crowds, forgetting to use safety devices, and generally entering into hazardous situations. Some subjects are extremely secretive and simply will not cooperate with those trying to ensure their safety. A system of protective services threatened in this fashion cannot operate effectively. Every time control of the situation is lost, individual safety is at risk. The individual who contributes to his own lack of security in this way is really in grave need of protection from himself. In the first place, it is necessary to educate him in the *need* for cooperating so as to assure his own security. There are some who simply do not understand what is required of them.[12] Effective protection is possible only when a sense of trust is developed between the individual protected and those responsible for his safety. In the second place, it may be necessary to impress upon the individual that measures cannot be taken *by others* to assure *his* security if he is not prepared to cooperate, as his lack of cooperation is likely to frustrate all measures designed to protect him. If the subject is important enough, he may have to be protected in spite of himself.[13].

Similarly, good security demands that there be no conscious or unconscious aiding of those who would harm the protected individual from within his own organization. The terrorist must be denied inside collaboration at all costs, for the presence of a Fifth Column can effectively destroy all measures of security based on an appreciation of an external threat only. High-risk targets often lead very involved lives, and those who are plotting to disrupt them in some way are in vital need of information concerning them in order to consummate their plans. The ability to acquire this information from an inside source is often indispensable to those who would harm the individual or his interests. Modern terrorist organizations systematically collect and stockpile such information, and it is constantly reviewed and updated.[14] Good security requires that such eventualities be foreclosed from the start, and efficient security procedures require a *thorough* screening of all persons coming into contact with the protected individual and his business and personal dealings. Good security procedures must always take into account the possible threat from within. Very often, when an individual appears to enjoy exceptionally good external security, the only option available for those who would harm him lies in penetrating his organization in some way. The assassination of Trotsky in Mexico in 1940 affords a very good example of the lengths to which persons will go to harm those who have apparently set up an impregnable protective security system. Efforts to kill Trotsky in his home failed on account of the effectiveness of his perimeter security, so the assassin insinuated himself into the Trotsky household where he was able to set himself up on familiar terms with his target.[15]

When the question is posed as to who is to be protected, the interests of the general public must not be ignored, even where the main threat is directed against a specific, high-risk individual. Members of the general public with whom the individual is associated in the normal course of his business or social life may well be exposed to abnormal risks as a result of this association. The risk is especially high where assassination by bombing in a public place is undertaken.[16] In Spain, in 1896, a bomb thrown by anarchists at establishment figures missed them but killed eleven and wounded forty in the crowd.[17] An individual who is traveling or performing in a public place, and is to be regarded as a high-risk target, may well bring upon innocent members of the public some sort of attack upon their persons or interests by reason only of his presence. Such considerations necessitate the closest cooperation between those assigned specifically to the personal protection of the individual and those having the larger law enforcement responsibilities involving the general public. Such a situation points up the need for continuing collaboration at all levels on the part of public and private law enforcement agencies.

In summary, *everybody* is in need of protection to some degree, but *some* are in need of more protection than others. The presence of a high-risk target, whether it be a human individual, a property, or a business interest, tends to attract danger to itself in a way that can affect persons who would not otherwise be regarded as security risks. There is a polarization of danger at certain times and in certain places. The presence of such high-risk targets imposes a particular strain upon the protective services set up to guard against the dangers involved and creates hazards that would not otherwise exist. The intensification factor must be understood and studied in detail before any scheme of protective services can be designed for the particular tasks involved.

NOTES
1. *Victims and Society* (Washington, D.C.: Visage Press, 1976), p. xiii.
2. In some countries, political violence is endimic. "In the

162 years since the assassination of Jean Jacques Dessalines of Haiti, over 30 rulers and former rulers of Latin American states have been murdered." Karl M. Schmitt, *Assassination and Political Violence,* Vol. 8, (Washington, D.C.: U.S. Government Printing Office, 1969), p. 537.

3. Thus, Fangio, the racing car driver, and di Stefano, the soccer player, were on different occasions kidnap victims.

4. "In all, American businesses abroad have been victimized by political terrorists more than 150 times in the last ten years, and, if anything, such incidents are likely to increase." *Newsweek,* November 14, 1977, p. 83.

5. As is the case presently, in Northern Ireland. Although target figures may be specifically chosen, there is also much random bombing and the general intent is to create an undifferentiating climate of fear.

6. Thus, to take, once more, Northern Ireland by way of illustration, Catholics, though relatively safe in their own residential areas, face great risks in Protestant areas and vice versa.

7. "...the psyche has the capacity to drive painful thoughts and feelings into unconsciousness where they are incapable of producing conscious pain or anxiety." Andrew Watson, *Psychiatry for Lawyers* (New York: International Universities Press, 1968), p. 94. "Executives and their corporate employers, are not equipped emotionally to deal with a constant 'state of seige'." Robert Lamborn, "Is Executive Protection Psycho-Therapy?" *Security Management,* January, 1978, pp. 54-55.

8. Multi-national corporations might be prepared to sustain quite large financial and material losses to terrorists rather than being forced out of business. On the other hand, relatively few executives killed or kidnapped might force a reappraisal of the policy of resistance.

9. "According to Government studies, over 1,100 executives have been killed in terrorist incidents since 1968. Hundreds of millions of dollars have been paid to meet kidnap demands for captured executives. Millions of dollars of corporate property and other assets have been expropriated by governments in retaliation against corporations who have bargained with terrorists. Corporations have been forced to reassess their operating

strategies in several South American and Middle Eastern Countries where terrorists are particularly active." Lloyd W. Singer and Jan Reber, "A New Way to Face Terrorists—a Crises Management System," *Security Management,* September, 1977, p. 6.

10. A big problem for the terrorist is credibility. His actions, if they are to impress, must be believable. For this reason, terrorists who have established a "track record" find it more easy to impress than those who have not.

11. "Terrorism is aimed at the people watching, not at the actual victims. Terrorism is theater." Brian Jenkins, "International Terrorism: A New Mode of Conflict," (Santa Monica, Cal.: Rand Corp., 1974), p. 4.

12. An interesting article in this respect is "Assassinations," John Williams, *Medico-Legal Journal,* 1965, pp. 93-100.

13. Politicians, in particular, tend to become very fatalistic in this regard and will often engage in extremely unwise behavior, such as mingling with crowds and seeking personal contact in a way that makes personal protection extremely difficult. Others will dismiss their escorts to gain some moments of privacy where they can relax. It is very difficult for bodyguards to disobey direct orders to leave from such subjects.

14. The amount of information that can be compiled by diligent researchers, even without extensive financial and other resources can be gaged from the results published, from time to time, by United States radical groups. Much of this information has been stockpiled and can be retrieved and disseminated quite rapidly.

15. See Isaac Don Levine, *The Mind of An Assassin* (New York: Farrar, Straus and Cudahy, 1959).

16. As witness the fate of Ronni Moffit, killed in the car bombing of Orlando Letelier, former Chilean Ambassador to the U.S., on September 22, 1976, at Sheridan Circle, Washington, D.C.

17. *The New York Times,* June 9, 1896.

Tactics of Terrorism

"The word 'terror' is so generally and universally used in connection with everyday trivial matters that it often fails to convey, when intended to do so, its real meaning.

Jim Corbett[1]

Protection Against What?

As already stated, the dangers against which protection is necessary have been deliberately expressed in comparatively narrow terms in the present text. The term "security" clearly embraces every aspect of safety to person, property, and other in terests;

but the protection necessary for an all encompassing view is beyond the scope of the present instruction and probably, on a realistic basis, beyond the scope of any work.[2] A clear limitation of objectives must be assigned at the start so that the magnitude of the task can be properly appreciated and a workable system of protective services established. For the present purposes, the threat to which the individual and his interests are exposed is conceived of as emanating from such violent and subversive groups as may be loosely comprehended within the term 'terror-istic." or which by reason of their imitation of the true terroristic enterprise can be categorized as "quasi-terroristic." While, in many ways, the structure and activities of such groups are anal-ogous to and make use of much the same means as those employed by ordinary criminal enterprises—particularly organ-ized crime—these latter, and the measures that must be taken against them to afford security of the individual and his inter-ests, are not part of the present text.[3] Protection, then, is con-ceived of in terms of the terroristic or quasi-terroristic threat to the individual, his property, and other interests, tangible and intangible. A thorough understanding of terrorism and quasi-terrorism is necessary, therefore, before any system of protec-tive services against these threats can be designed.

There is no completely satisfactory definition of terrorism, particularly in an international forum.[4] Efforts by distinguished scholars and international bodies alike have failed to produce agreement on the essential elements of such a definition. There are many reasons for this, but the main one is that what is com-monly described as "terrorism" contains a judgmental factor on which there is ample room for disagreement on political, ideo-logical, and moral grounds.[5] Bearing in mind the lack of perhaps the best definition that can be adopted for the present purposes is that offered by the National Advisory Committee Task Force on Disorders and Terrorism:[6]

> Terrorism is a tactic or technique by means of
> which a violent act or the threat thereof is used for
> the prime purpose of creating overwhelming fear
> for coercive purposes.

There are many common crimes of which fear is an incidental element. In terroristic crimes the fear itself is of overriding importance to the ultimate objective.[7]

More important than any precise definition of terrorism is an understanding of its constitutive elements. It is less important to know what it is than what it does to people, property, and other interests. *Terrorism is intimidatory.* It is intended to affect the conduct and thinking not only of the human beings against whom the violent act, or the threat of the violent act, is directed but also others who are meant to be influenced by even the remotest consequences. There is, thus, a principal victim; namely, the person against whom the act or threat is immediately directed and an ulterior victim, which may be society itself or a substantial segment of it. If businessmen are kidnapped, others get the message. So do their families and friends. *Terrorism is always purposeful.* Even the most sense-less and barbaric of acts, such as indiscriminate bombings, have a definite objective. Indeed, the more random and indis-criminate the choice of the victim, the more terrifying are the consequences. Sometimes, that objective is the creation of a generalized fear and confusion in the community.[8] No one knows who might be the next victim. At other times, the pur-pose is deliberately obscured by the direction of the violence. Even where the violence is clearly random and appears to have no discernible pattern, the objectives of those who are direct-ing it are usually recognizable upon careful analysis. *Terrorism is intended to act upon the minds of human individuals.* Terror-ism (as distinct from terror) is a purely human creation.[9] It is produced by humans for humans. The activities comprising terrorism are therefore connected, with *human sentiment* and *human values.* The terrorist attacks that which he believes to be of value to the person whose conduct he wishes to influence. This is a fundamental dynamic of terrorism, the principal reason why it is effective at all. People are kidnapped, for example, because of their intrinsic worth, and because others will do something to get them back. Were this not so, kidnapping would be pointless. *Terrorism is, by nature, a sustained activity.* While isolated acts having the characteristics of terrorism are perfectly possible—and, indeed, not infrequent—the notion of intimidation and coercion generally implies a persistent cam-paign over a period designed to influence those against whom it is directed. While Terrorism takes many forms and employs many modalities, the essence of this activity is to be found in the creation of the coercive fear that it produces rather than in the other consequences of the act. Terroristic crimes are a means rather than an end in themselves. While, therefore, murder and assassination may be terroristic modalities, they are distinguished from the ordinary criminal forms by reference to the ulterior consequences desired by those who employ them.[10] *Acts and threats of terrorism are designed to serve as a warning.* The immediate victim is held up as a horrible example to others so that there might be a change in conduct or attitude by the survivors.[11] Terrorism is a weapon in the overall power struggle and is designed to secure control through domination of the human mind by fear. *Terrorism is divisive.* It is intended to operate on individual minds and attack groups so as to cause doubt and chaos. Some people are more easily frightened than others. Terrorism works on the most fearful in the hope of weakening the resolve of those who would otherwise stand up to it. *Terrorism is clandestine by nature;* that is, the activities themslves are plotted and planned in secret and only reveal themselves in the execution phase. Terrorists need a safe base from which to operate and a safe base to which to return. The terrorist, therefore, has the advantage of *surprise and initiative* and all protective systems must be designed to take account of this characteristic. *Terrorism, at least in its inception, is a highly impersonal activity.* This means that the immediate victim is de-personalized as much as possible so as to produce the maximum fear and uncertainty, and also to permit those who have to under-take these gruesome activities a measure of personal and psychological insulation from what they have to do.[12] This is particularly the case in kidnapping and hostage takings where terrorists might have close contact with their victims over an extended period of time. For this reason, much terrorism is idealized or ideologically justified. There is an evident denial of reality in this that makes those who undertake these tasks on an operational level extremely difficult to deal with.

The exponents of terrorism employ a variety of means, tactics and techniques to attain their objectives. Their relative degree of success in each case depends upon the impact of what is used not only upon the target figures themselves but also upon the ulterior audience that they are intended to impress. Terroristic activities can be divided broadly into two groups. The first group comprises those actions that are immediately and dramatically destructive of human life and property and are intended to generate fear simply on that account. Such activities include assassinations, bombings, sabotage, and other *purely destructive acts*. Protective systems, to be effective, must therefore have a high preventive capacity designed to frustrate the commission of the act. The second category comprises those acts that merely place human individuals or property in extreme jeopardy so as to set up not merely a fearful reaction in others but a *bargaining situation* that the terrorist or his organization can turn to account. Foremost among these are kidnappings and hostage takings. Protective measures must comprise not only a preventive response, but also a capability of dealing with the secondary effects so as to be able to rescue the victim from the predicament in which he has been placed. Purely destructive acts are the hardest against which to erect any form of effective protection. If the action is successful, little is left to do to save lament. Those that are designed to set up a bargaining situation are generally susceptible to influence not merely by the original protective measures designed to safeguard against them but, in the event of a failure of these, there is generally a second opportunity to save the ultimate harm that can befall the victim.

Effective protection is only possible where the threat is seen and appreciated in its proper perspective. Unless the true nature of the threat is properly determined from the outset, the protective system erected against it will be inadequately oriented. Hence, the importance of knowing, in detail, exactly what is ranged against the protective system to be developed. There is great danger in underestimating or mistaking the nature of the potential harm to which the individuals to be protected are exposed. Protective measures can be completely vitiated by choosing the wrong form of protection against anticipated dangers. A system designed only to prevent the individual from being ambushed between his home and office will not afford much protection against his being poisoned, or, indeed, against any of a multitude of harms an evil imagination might conjure up. The assessment of risk is, therefore, a highly skilled task and should be undertaken with the proper degree of experience and the best available data. *Security analysis is only as good as the data on which it is based.*[13] If this is of poor quality or is deficient, an accurate estimation of the threat will not emerge and the protective system designed as a result will be defective.

The capability and expertise of different terrorist groups varies widely. Many of these groups, in different parts of the world, now have a long operational history. The last few years have shown a remarkable improvement in terrorist tactics and techniques, and undoubtedly there has been a high degree of technology transfer and some common training among the various transnational groups.[14] Political terrorists are generally well trained and dedicated. They will have done their homework well, and their actions consistently show a high degree of professional planning and preparation. This, coupled with the natural advantages of surprise and initiative, make them a formidable proposition. They are often well supplied with money and other material resources. The ability of such a group to carry out even the most audacious operations should never be underestimated. Their financial and other strengths are translated not only into excellent weaponry and other equipment, but also into the means to purchase information, penetrate organizations and develop false identities. As a general rule, it should always be assumed that the quality of the planning and preparation by terrorist groups of a professional nature will be at least as good as that of the forces opposing them.

In summary, then, the principal threat against which protection must be established is one posed by highly trained and motivated individuals often having a tight organizational structure upon which to rely and having the advantages of surprise and initiative. Such opponents of the system will generally be well supplied with the material means to effect the harm they intend to cause and will not be lacking in resources. They will attempt to secure all necessary information to enable them to carry out their designs, and they will execute their plans with purpose and determination. The protective services designed to ensure the security of the individual and group interests thus put at risk must take into account all these factors and must have adequate resources and personnel available to meet the threat. A system developed to meet such professionally developed dangers should, if it has the requisite flexibility, have little difficulty in offering substantial protection against opportunistic harm from other sources.

NOTES

1. *Man-Eaters of India* (New York: Oxford University Press, 1957), p. 11. Sir Robert Thompson in his *Defeating Communist Insurgency* (New York: Praeger, 1966), p. 9, writes: "If I had to produce a bibliography, it would be headed by a

book no one else would include: *The Man-Eating Leopard of Rudraprayag* (New York: Oxford University Press, 1947) by the late Jim Corbett (and his *Man-Eaters of the Kumaon,* Oxford Press, 1944). This provides an excellent example of a vast area of countryside under the terrorist control of a man-eating leopard, showing the effect on the lives of the people and of the pilgrims who passed through the area, and describes the painstaking methods required to deal with the threat."

2. It is for this reason that general textbooks on "security" can do no more than give a rather superficial overview of a very broad subject. Security is not a subject that lends itself to introductory writings.

3. For the similarities with organized crime, see *The Challenge of Crime in a Free Society* (Washington, D.C.: U.S. Government Printing Office, 1967), pp. 187-209.

4. "After five years, there were still no satisfactory answers. No one had a definition of terrorism." J. Bowyer Bell, "Trends on Terror," XXIX *World Politics,* April, 1977, no. 3, p. 481.

5. On this, see H.H.A. Cooper, "Terrorism: The Problem of the Problem of Definition." 25 *Chitty's Law Journal,* January, 1978.

6. *Disorders and Terrorism* (Washington, D.C.: U.S. Government Printing Office, 1976), p. 3.

7. The fear generated in terroristic crimes is an end itself. The use to which the fear so generated is put, is *terrorism.*

8. Of urban terrorism it has been written: "The activities of such groups do not involve merely policemen, soldiers, diplomats and officials. On the contrary, they are designed to kill ordinary people. The purpose of terrorism is to terrorize. When a child is caught in their crossfire or a worker killed by a bomb, their deaths represent not 'mistakes' but an integral part of the business of terror." Anthony Burton, *Urban Terrorism* (New York: The Free Press, 1976), p. 5.

9. Terror may be induced accidentally or by natural causes. It is an emotion or state of mind, which may be individual or collective. It is the use to which this *purposefully* induced condition is put that constitutes terrorism.

10. This is best seen by looking at those crimes where terror is certainly generated, but is not made use of by the perpetrator for the accomplishment of his overall design. Thus, the

so-called "Son of Sam" certainly terrorized a large part of New York City during 1976-77, but the creation of this state of intense fear was incidental to his purposes which were to satisfy certain unexplained internal needs.

11. Roland Gaucher expressed it thus: "The goal of terrorism is not to kill or destroy property but to break the spirit of the opposition. A minister is assassinated; his successor takes warning. A policeman is killed; ten others tremble." *The Terrorists* (London: Secker and Warburg, 1968), p. 298.

12. It is generally easier to kill a stranger than one with whom there has been some human interaction. It is easier to kill from a distance, preferably without personal knowledge of the victims. Personalized killings take a powerful motivation capable of overriding ordinary considerations of humanity.

13. Idries Shah, "A response based upon inadequate data is not a response," *Reflections,* Penguin Books, 1972, p. 60.

14. The CIA report, *International Terrorism in 1976,* RP77-10034U, July, 1977, p. 3, records factors that ". . . [all] document the trend toward greater cooperation among terrorists of different nationalities that has been observable for several years."

Assassinations

"...*Prince Eugene expressed his astonishment that Charles XII was willing to take the risk of travelling without an Austrian armed escort in a country 'where one can find men who for a 30 sol piece would fire a musket at him from a hedge.'*"

R.M. Hatton[1]

Assassination is a very special type of intentional homicide.
The term "assassination", like terrorism, is of somewhat controversial definition. Nevertheless, unlike the case of terrorism,
there is general agreement on the nature and application of the
term; what is in some disagreement is its width or elasticity. The
real problem lies in the fact that the word is often very loosely
and inappropriately used.[2] It is a word that, in ordinary parlance,
carries a very heavy emotional load, a load of fear that characteristically lends itself to the terroristic purpose. For this reason,
it is sometimes used where the killing is of a particularly frightful, sudden or unexpected nature; and the reporter of the event
wishes to emphasize these characteristics. As with terrorism,
however, there is little point in getting hung up on the semantics
of the matter. It is better to know the constitutive elements of
assassination than to be overly preoccupied with the niceties of
definition. Definition is important mainly for purposes of communication, so that people may be sure they are all talking about
the same thing. Once more, it is emphasized, however, that it is
essential that there be the fullest comprehension of the true
nature of this type of criminal activity in order that the appropp-
riate protective measures can be taken. For the present purposes, the following definition is offered.

> *Assassination is the willful killing by a human*
> *being of another human being with the object of*
> *affecting the course of events through the remo-*
> *val of that individual from the sphere of influence*
> *that he would normally occupy.*

Whatever the hidden, private motivation of the assassin may be,
however distorted and removed from reality his thinking, the act
of assassination is always undertaken with some ostensible
public purpose in view. It contrasts, notably, with the purely private killing intended to resolve some conflict between two indi-

viduals, manifest or otherwise. This is the most distinctive feature of assassination. For this reason, the object of assassination will usually be some public figure or some individual engaged in the exercise of a prominent public function. This is not to suggest that public figures are never killed for private reasons, but only that this distinction is important to any definition of assassination. *Assassination has a symbolic quality* about it that is important to the actor and the cause he serves. In almost all cases, despite the peculiar, often distorted motivation of the assassins—many of whom are significantly mentally disturbed[3]—the killings themselves are generally of an *impersonal character*; and it is the office or function that is being attacked rather than the person who, for the time being, occupies it. Thus, assassination seems to have an exceptionally callous, indifferent quality that both heightens the fearfulness of the act and colors the reputation of the assassin. This is often the case where the victim is a head of state or a prominent executive of some other kind. Dictionary definitions usually stress the secret and particularly treacherous nature of assassination.[4] Taken in its literal sense, this element is somewhat misleading. This notion is generally derived from the historical associations upon which the term itself is said to have been based. The Hashshashin were Twelfth Century Moslem zealots trained to undertake political killings under the influence of a combination of drugs and religion.[5] Modern assassinations do not always bear this secret character. There will, as in the case of all terrorism, be a covert or clandestine aspect in the planning and preparation phase, but the killing itself will often be marked by a notable public display of violence intended to impress and create great fear. Often the assassin will take great risks to achieve this end, although the killing could have been done more efficiently without so much attention focused upon it. The secret and treacherous aspects of assassination are, however, quite evident in some killings, as, for example, that of the assassination in December 1973 of the Spanish Premier, Admiral Luis Carrero Blanco, by means of a subterranean bomb that was clandestinely placed in the pathway of his car and detonated with tremendous force.[6] Many assassinations are carried out in public places by unknown assailants who make their escape in the resulting confusion. It is all much more a matter of tactics and technique than a mere semantic necessity for the purposes of structuring this concept. *Assassinations are always deliberate and premeditated.* Sometimes, however, the wrong target is selected or, in the course of the action, the wrong individual is dispatched. This is exemplified by the famous M'Naghten case which gave rise in 1843 to the common law rules governing insanity in criminal cases. M'Naghten had intended to assassinate Sir Robert Peel, the British Prime Minister, but through mistaken identity killed his private secretary instead.[7] This is an operational fault rather than one connected with the planning and preparation of the event. *There are no accidental assassinations.* There may be accidental killings of public figures, but the very notion of assassination depends upon its willful character.[8] Another distinctive feature of assassinations is the unusual *determination and vigor* with which they are pressed home. The target has usually been selected with great care and for specific purposes. Very often, the target will be heavily protected at all times, and the attack can only be successful if it is capable of penetrating the successive rings of protection with which the subject is surrounded. This fact is usually well known to the attacker and is taken into account by him, producing a tremendous amount of force which is generated by the effort of effecting the necessary penetration and overcoming the resistance so as to attain the objective. This frequently—in unprofessional killings—gives the assassination a suicidal or kamikaze-like character. The individual undertaking the mission virtually writes off his own existence as part of the price of success. This phenomenon is most usually observable in cases involving idealistic or ideologically motivated killers of whom the Nineteenth Century Anarchists are the classic example.[9] These facts leave the attacker very vulnerable at the precise moment of pressing home his assault on the protected figure so that he relies heavily upon the advantages that surprise and initiative confer upon him. He will need to be fairly close at the crucial moment in order to begin his attack with any prospect of success. Those experienced in providing protective services can, however, contribute a large measure of safety to the target figure by recognizing the signs of nervous agitation in the assassin that are preparatory to the making of the actual assault.[10] *The target of assassination is generally chosen with some care and for very definite reasons.* The killer's purpose would not be served by the death of another victim. The choice does not, therefore, admit alternatives. Not unnaturally, mistakes will be made from time to time by the assassins, and the wrong target will be victim of the attack. Mayor Cermak of Chicago was killed by Guiseppe Zangara whose intended, and only, target was President-elect Franklin D. Roosevelt.[11] This is, however, a fault in the execution and not a result of pre-selected alternatives or contingency planning. Again, former Governor Connally was an accidental victim in the assassination of President John F. Kennedy and not an alternative selected in case it had not been possible to assassinate the President. Such mistakes or faulty execution really change the whole character of the crime. If an alternative target has to be selected at the last moment or is inadvertently hit in the course of the attack on the principal target figure, the assassination attempt proper can be said to have failed. *Assassination candidates are not generally targets of opportunity.*[12] In most cases, the assassin or members of his team will have stalked the target figure for some time and will be thoroughly familiar with his movements, habits, dress and other important factors that have to be taken into account.[13] The mode and means of assassination will be chosen accordingly. The main point that must be constantly borne in mind with regard to assassinations is that it seems to those acting that the removal of the individual in question will have a significant impact on the events or designs they are influencing. This appears to be the case even where the assassin is clearly mentally disturbed.[14] The true impact of the target figure upon events and real extent of his influence may well have been exaggerated, but the assassination choice is made upon the basis of appearances. It is for this reason that the keeping of a low profile is often recommended as a defensive measure. As the importance of the target is reduced the likelihood of assassination often recedes.

Assassination has an admonitory character. It is intended to serve as a warning to others; and, consequently, the way in which the assassination is carried out is often as important as the event itself. Thus, risks are often taken so as to leave a particular impression or "trademark." Assassination carries an unmistakable message.

Because of the peculiar characteristics of assassination that have been mentioned, it is usually possible in a broad, general way to foretell who might be a likely candidate for assassination. Certain conditions have to be fulfilled before an individual can be seen as a potential victim.[15] *Assassinations are not randomly undertaken.* The target is carefully chosen for a specific, though not immediately evident, reason. There is a certain logic to assassination which, if it can be detected and understood, affords useful predictors to the behavior and methods of the assassin. Although prediction can often only be undertaken in the grossest fashion, it does assist those entrusted with the security of individuals the opportuniy to identify their high-risk targets and the nature and areas of their vulnerability. Those who are engaged in the protection of individuals believed to constitute a high assassination risk will find it a useful exercise to think like assassins. How would I assassinate X if I were assigned the task? This will enable a review to be made of the protective measures that have been taken and to spot the weak points in them that would be naturally favorable to an assassin. It will also enable some appreciation to be made of the means and methods that a potential assassin would choose. Defense against assassination is greatly facilitated by getting into the mind of the assassin and thinking ahead of him. Countermeasures to frustrate *his* plans can then be developed, and he can be forced into alternative patterns of action which are less favorable to the attainment of his objectives. *The first step in the protection against assassination is the identification and evaluation of potential assassination victims in order that appropriate steps may be taken to safeguard them.* From the perspective of the terrorist, assassination carries many advantages over other forms of action. In the first place, *it is spectacular.* Assassination has a dreadful symbolism about it. The assassination of a public figure, particularly one who is heavily guarded, carries a fearful message to the whole community.[16] When successful, it can cause great confusion and a strange type of social paralysis. If leaders and prominent figures can be eliminated in this way, it minimizes the feeling of security of all. Assassination, if the target is well chosen, can have a dramatically destabilizing effect.[17] Additionally, those who are in a more immediate relationship to the victim are made fearful for their own safety, while those who might succeed him in his functions are threatened in a very specific and forceful way. The reactions of Vice President Lyndon Johnson on learning of the death of President Kennedy are most instructive in this regard.[18] *Assassination is a final and irrevocable solution.* It is a solution that does not admit of any half measures and represents a very definite step for those who take it. Where great emotion and regard surround the life and work of the individual assassinated, this final removal of his personal influence from the scene of activity can have direct and dramatic effects upon the course of events. It brings about a sudden and abrupt curtailment not only of the life of the individual but also of the policies and practices that he represents. This is particularly so where the victim is a prominent political figure, and his removal would lead not merely to a change of policies but, perhaps, to a change of government as well.[19] From the terrorists' perspective, *assassination is relatively easy to undertake.* If it is carefully planned and the right opportunity is sought, it is a much easier operation to carry out than many others that terrorists would have to engage in to achieve the same degree of impact. The prospect of assassination offers the terrorist a wide choice of means, and he is able to adapt these to the purposes of his undertaking. For example, it may be easier to poison certain victims than to shoot them. On the other hand, too, the means can be readily adapted to the ends so that an important political statement is made thereby. There are ample opportunites for engaging in a direct, confrontation-type situation such as a shooting at close range or a stabbing; or, alternatively, the victim can be dealt with at a comparatively long-range by the use of appropriate weaponry or explosives. The number of alternatives is considerable; and it is thus important, from a protective services perspective, to reduce these alternatives by appropriate countermeasures. In addition, this type of terroristic activity is *relatively economical.* It does not, ordinarily, take a large number of operatives to engage in assassination, whatever the means chosen; and there are fewer of the logistical problems that are involved in other types of terroristic activity where it is necessary to keep the victim alive for bargaining purposes. A kidnapping requires, generally, not only a great deal more by way of preparation, communications, and the availability of safe locations, but also arrangements for keeping the victim alive and hidden from the authorities over a long period of time. This is not only costly in material resources, but requires a larger number of operatives than those required for the direct assassination. Because of these factors the latter operation is less sensitive to the techniques of counterintelligence.[20] There is an additional consideration that is worthy of note. Assassination can, on account of its nature, be undertaken as a "contract job." The individual who is assigned to the removal of the target figure by these means need have nothing but a mercenary relationship with those who have planned and prepared the assassination. The assassin may, therefore, be a professional who is operating quite dispassionately, in this matter, for gain; and this consideration will give the whole character of the assassination a very serious turn for those having protective responsibilities. The more coldbloodedly and detachedly the assassination can be undertaken, the more likely it is to succeed and the more difficult it will be to investigate, for such an assassin carries no burden of guilt, and is unlikely to leave clues or assist, even unwittingly, in his own apprehension.[21] On the contrary, every endeavor will be made to ensure that the assassin is never apprehended or even known. Organized crime killings and those undertaken by government operatives are models in this respect.

Protection against the possibility of assassination is, perhaps, the most difficult task of all for those engaged in assuring personal safety. *A determined, patient, and resourceful killer will be able to penetrate almost any security system.* Even the threat of assassination notably alters the quality of life for the potential victim. He is no longer able to engage freely in activities that a normal person takes for granted, and the stress of maintaining alertness and a different kind of lifestyle may seriously affect the individual's health and enjoyment of life. The private as well as the public functions of the person threatened may suffer severe curtailment. Indeed, if the threat is sufficiently intense, the objective of the assassin may well be attained by indirect means. Under certain conditions, stress alone can kill.[22] Additionally, the cost of the most thorough protection that can be afforded is bound to be extremely high; and the cost, even for the most wealthy, represents a substantial drain upon their resources. *No individual can ever be made absolutely safe from the possibility of assassination, and the knowledge that this is so produces strange and unwanted effects.* In some extreme cases, it induces in the potential victim a severe case of paranoia so that even close friends and associates are suspected of causing harm or desiring to cause harm to the individual concerned. Even those engaged in protecting the potential victim come under the heaviest cloud of suspicion and if the individual were an autocratic government figure, for example, this could lead to frequent changes of favor, outbursts of rage, and other unpleasant consequences for all concerned.[23] This eventuality must be taken into account expecially in the case of visiting dignitaries and others from overseas whose authority is unlimited and whose resolution of their own security problems is untroubled by the normal considerations limiting persons in this country. Such abnormal emotions are not restricted to foreign potentates, however, and, in greater or lesser degree, this factor has to be taken into account in every case. The fear induced by a threat of death which is constantly present is transformed and projected onto those who are closest to the potential target figure. Sometimes these fears are justified and the proper precautions would be justified on a close examination of the matter, but the phenomena of paranois is an important consideration that must be allowed for in planning any protective system. It has been emphasized that a system of protective services is dependent for its effectivenss upon a large measure of trust, a relationship of confidence in those who are undertaking the protection of the individual concerned. Unless this trust exists, the whole system of protective services is inevitably weakened. Trust is always eroded by feelings of paranoia in any degree and where these are induced, even for realistic reasons, they are likely to frustrate efforts to protect the individual from harm.

Protection against assassination must be methodically and thoroughly developed. This requires a systematic study of every facet of the behavior, habits, attitudes, and functions of the indentified potential victim; a thorough study of those persons who are likely to perpetrate harm by way of assassination upon the person being protected; and a study of the means available to such persons and their likely employment having regard to all the personal and environmental factors involved. It is highly desirable that such an analysis be conducted by experienced, qualified personnel who will not, necessarily, have the operational responsibilities of putting into effect the countermeasures to be designed. These are essentially different functions and require the exercise of different skills. A person who might be an excellent bodyguard, having all the characteristics and abilities required for assuring the physical safety of the person to be protected, might not have the skills necessary to conduct a sophisticated analysis of the type necessary to ensure good protective planning. Where these tasks are appropriately separated, there needs to be a thorough integration of the two functions. Protective planning is a very exacting task requiring a thorough knowledge of all the practical aspects that are involved. It is not a task for which academic or classroom experience alone is sufficint. The individual engaged in such planning should have considerable operational and field experience in order to be able to engage effectively in the more theoretical aspects of this task. Nevertheless, he should be free from the practical execution of these operational aspects, and he should have an observer's detached appreciation of them rather than being an active participant in putting them into effect. Additionally, the different aspects of planning of the protective response will call for a variety of skills that are rarely to be found reposing in a single individual. The design of the most effective system of protective security is, necessarily, *a team effort*, with the proper utilization of the skills afforded by different disciplines being directed by a single individual who thoroughly understands what each discipline can contribute. The extent to which these various contributions can be made will depend upon the available in-house resources, but where the risk of harm is seen to be great—yet the possibility of designing effective protection against it is slight by reason of a lack of experience or specialist knowledge—it may be as well to engage the services or specialist knowlege—it may be as well to engage the services of the appropriate specialists who are able to undertake the task more adequately. There are many areas in which the employment of specialists might be wise. In particular, threat analysis is a highly specialized task, the abilities for which are confined to relatively few individuals. It may well add greatly to the security of the individuals being protected if the services of such persons ae retained on an "as needed" basis to supplement the available in-house ability. *However this division of labor is effected, it is essential that there be proper coordination between those who are planning the protective response and those who are engaged in providing the operational protection to the ptoential victim.*[24]

It cannot be overemphasized that the proper protection of the individual demands a most exact and detailed knowledge of every facet of his personality, his habits, and his activities.The measure of this knowledge determines, from the outset, the effectiveness of the protective system that can be developed. There is a direct correlation between this basic data and the protective measures that can be adopted. There is an understandable—but unfortunate—reluctance on the part of many individuals to confide to the fullest extent in those who are to protect them, and the amount of information that will be made available on this account will, almost always, be related to the magnitude of the perceived threat. As the individual comes to feel himself threatened in a very direct and immediate way, he will ordinarily be more cooperative with those who are seeking the information necessary to protect him. It may well be too late at that stage. It will inevitably be the case, however, that the fullest and most complete information will not come directly from the individual protected, and such as he does make available will thus have to be supplemented with information from other sources. *It should always be borne in mind that while those undertaking the protection of the individual under threat of assassination are gathering their own information concerning him, those seeking to do him harm will be undertaking a like exercise.*[25] They will be attempting, as thoroughly as possible, to build up their own dossier in order to be able to develop their own assassination plans effectively. It is often the greatest tragedy that those who might have afforded protection are denied or are unable to secure material information that is obtained by those seeking to harm the individual being protected. It is always a good argument with such persons to point out that the information available to those desirous of causing harm might well be more extensive than that available to those entrusted with the protective functions *unless the subject himself is willing to cooperate on the fullest and freest of bases.* The uncertainties of human life and the continually changing patterns of human existence will almost certainly render much information in the possession of the protective forces obsolete within a relatively short while. The same is true of information available to the assassins, but they will handle that problem after their own fashion. *Information must be constantly updated,* and the system must have an inherent flexibility that allows for change of plans according to the whims and caprices of the individuals being protected. Busy men are not always mindful of the needs of those entrusted with their security. Information concerning the subject to be protected should always be as complete and up-to-date as possible and should be in a form that can be readily processed and disseminated to those having the operational responsibilities. These responsibilities can only be adequately discharged if the protective forces are aware of what the individual to be protected is likely to do, where he is likely to go, how he is likely to react under different circumstances, and what changes in the ordinary pattern of his activity can be anticipated over the requisite period of time. Where protection has to be arranged for many on a relatively impersonal basis, this obviously calls for a very sophisticated operation with considerable division of labor.

In the planning and preparation stage it cannot be overemphasized that there is no subsitute for hard intelligence. This applies to the private as much as the public sector. If the plans for an assassination are known in sufficient detail, steps can be taken either to vary the itinerary or activities of the subject to be protected or to ensure that an effective measure of protection is taken against the apprehended threat. Additionally, appropriate moves can be taken against those who intend to attempt the assassination so as to frustrate the commission of the crime. The establishment and operation of an efficient intelligence network will often supply such hard information. A system of obtaining reliable information is a most worthwhile investment. The value of the information is, however, limited by the organizational arrangements for its dissemination to those who can take effective action in consequence of it. There must always be an effective linkage between the organization responsible for the gathering, processing and storage of all intelligence, and the dissemination of it to the operational elements engaged in the provision of physical protection. In most cases, however, the protection to be afforded will not be based upon hard intelligence of this sort. The threat will be general, and any assessment of it will be largely speculative and dependent upon the quality of the input fed into the system and the technique utilized in processing.[26] There is a real value in imaginative, creative speculation, but it ought never be allowed to become a subsitute for hard factual information. There is always the danger, too, of creating unnecessary fears by such activity, and this must be guarded against so as not to generate paranoia in the protected subject. Where there is no hard information concerning a specific assassination attempt, and there is no identified assassin against who protective measures can be set up, it is necessary to work on a general threat analysis in order to be able to establish an effective system of protective services against the assessed prospects of such a general eventuality.[27] The limitations of general threat analysis should be clearly understood, and measures taken in accordance with what might be suggested by the results of such analysis should be seen as being in the nature of *insurance against harm.*

Successful assassination depends to a very large extent upon opportunity. While the perfect opportunity can rarely be manufactured, the elements of it can, often with the victim's unconscious assistance. The assassin in his planning and preparation sets up a *theoretical opportunity* which, if it materializes, he will be in position to take advantage of in order to complete his mission successfully, Those engaged in the planning and provision of protective services are concerned, to a large extent, with denying the assassin this opportunity, or modifying it in such a way as to frustrate *his* planning and preparation as well as denying him the opportunities of alternative action. *Opportunity, so far as assassination is concerned, is largely a function of time and place.* It is a question of question of getting the target individual in the right place, at the right time, for the harmful influences to be effective against his person.[28] The target individual's intentions and movements will have been observed and the planning and preparation for the act itself will proceed on the basis of the potential victim being in a particular place at a particular time where the chosen means of this assassination can be effectively brought to bear upon his person.[29] *Stable routines facilitate assassinations*, as indeed they do any other type of act directed against the person. Such planning and preparation by the assassin or his accomplices are greatly facilitated where the individual is of regular habits and is known to be in a particular location at a particular time. Such regularity of activity not only provides greater opportunities for planning and preparation but also affords. In the moment of execution, a more stable target for the assassin. *The successful assassination is a best use of the opportunity presented.* Time is an essential factor in most cases. Many opportunities are of extremely short duration.[30] Sometimes an assassination is successfully carried out by an emotionally disturbed person who has merely taken advantage of a casual opportunity which presented itself. Yet even in these cases the assassin had to prepare himself to be ready to take advantage of this opportunity as it occurred.[31] More usually, the opportunity will have been carefully planned to occur and will be based on certain assumptions as to its probable occurrence, made as a result of preparatory study of the subject to be assassinated, his habits and environment. The assassin, or those with whom he is associated, will engage in the appropriate long-term, long-range surveillance of the target. If they do their job well, they will become thoroughly familiar with his general habits and even the most intimate details of his personality. They will also take careful note of the protective measures designed to safeguard the target figure. If he is escorted from his residence, for example, they will know exactly how this is done, the number and position of bodyguards, the times and mode of arrival of vehicles, the way they are placed, as well as all the other factors necessary to be taken into account in the operations. They may have to move in for a closer range surveillance and even try practice exercises to test the feasibility of the planning operations in which they are engaged in relation to the actual attempt. *There can be no absolute protection against the opportunistic attack.* If the attacker is in the right position, at the right time, with the right weapons, there will be only the physical security ring interposed between him and the target. If his planning and preparation have been effective he will be able to penetrate this and carry out his mission. Only a purely accidental circumstance or a failure on his own part can defeat him at such a juncture in the execution.

The way in which the assassination is to be carried out will depend on a large number of factors. It will depend, in the first place, upon an assessment of the opportunity factors and of the strength of the protective elements which have been provided for the security of the prospective target figure. At times, however, the objectives of the assassin and those with whom he is associated may dictate the way in which the mission is carried out. In some cases, for example, it may be desirable that the assassination be seen to take on the character of an accident, while in others the maximum publicity for the group engaged in the assassination may be a prime requisite so that not only the event, but the way it was engineered, must receive the fullest illumination.[32] In the latter eventually, it may be necessary for the assassination to be carried out in the most public way possible and using the most spectacular means so as to attract publicity. In yet other cases, there may be some hidden motive requiring that others be blamed for the death of the individual concerned so that the assassination is carefully carried out with the view to implicating these other parties. This is often the case where the means used are covert, such as poisoning, or a hidden explosive charge. Especially in the case of terrorist groups, there is almost invariably a propaganda value attached to an assassination which will, of itself, determine the way in which it is to be carried out. The more complicated the plan chosen, and the purposes for which the assassination is being undertaken, the greater the risk to the operative who will be carrying it out and the greater the risk of the plan becoming known before it can be put into effect. *Generally speaking, the simpler the plan, the greater the chances of success.* Where the objective of assassination is simply the elimination of the individual rather than an additional profiting from the event in some way, the protective tasks are greatly increased.

Where the individual is to be killed is, again, in the first place, largely a matter of opportunity. Place can, however, in some cases, be quite as important as time. It may be that surveillance of the individual, his habits and the degree of protection he customarily receives, has indicated that he is more vulnerable in some places than others. The nature of the surveillance and the operational planning will depend, to a large extent, upon the stability of the individual's movements and the ease with which they can be determined and predicted. This is a most important built-in safety factor, for the time and patience of the assassin are also limited. If the individual, for example, is in the habit of leaving his residence at a fixed time each day and returning to it also at a fixed time each day, whereas movements in between those times are irregular and unpredictable, it may well be that the character and timing of the assassination will be determined by the need to take advantage of the opportunity afforded by his relatively regular patterns of leaving and returning to his residence.[33] Where the assassin's resources are small his own flexibility will be limited. Where the assassination is concerned with the making of a particular statement or a certain public impact, the determination will be according to the needs of the operation regardless of ease of opportunity. If, for example, it is necessary for policy purposes to carry out the assassination in a public place, then opportunity must be made, rather than simply taken advantage of, by reference to its own existence. The victim will not be killed in the most favorable place for the assassin, but the enhanced risks will be commensurate with what are seen as the essential goals.[34] Security factors and the general vulnerability of the victim will be taken into account and, unless it is the objective of the assassin to demonstrate his own prowess in effecting a particularly difficult killing, or to make some particular political statement thereby, then it will generally be the case that the place of the assassination will be chosen on the grounds of the ease with which the mission can be conducted. The more lightly guarded the individual is, the more likely he is to be attacked *at that point in time and place.* Once the individual has been chosen as a target, this is the consideration most likely to determine the nature of the operation. For example, if it is determined as a result of surveillance that body-guards are regularly relieved at certain hours, or are less alert at certain times and in certain places than at others, the competent assassin will attempt to undertake his mission in accordance with those observations.[35] *Assassins look for the weak points in the system.* If they really mean to do the job, they look for whatever circumstances will aid them. They take advantage of whatever opportunity presents itself if they are unable to create their own. *Good protection is based on a planned reduction opportunities.*

Where the assassination is to be attempted will determine in a large measure how it is to be undertaken; namely, the methods to be used and the equipment and techniques that will be necessary to undertake the task. Assassination is not simply the killing of a human being; it is the killing of a chosen individual, in a significant way, and in a particular historical context. Weaponry is an important consideration in this matter. For a successful assassination to be carried out, the weaponry must be suitable for the time, the place, and the task. It must also be adapted to the situation and the special purposes of the assassin and his associates. If the death is to appear on the stage of history as accidental or due to natural causes, then the assassination cannot be undertaken with a weapon that would not ordinarily be used or could not possibly be attributed to those who are to be blamed; that part of the mission will fail, notwithstanding that the victim is eliminated. The greatest attention must be paid in detail to these matters if the operation is to be completely successful. Such considerations are of prime importance where the assassination is part of a planned *coup d'etat* or is carried out by government operatives for political purposes.[36] The difficulties of coordinating all these details in the more complicated types of assassination afford the individual against whom they are directed a certain precarious built-in security. It is not a security upon which, however, a great deal of reliance can be placed, for too many imponderables are involved. The means to be employed will also, in large measure, determine the character and capabilities of the assassin. An assassin who is only familiar with certain types of firearms will not use others. This is particularly the case with professional or mercenary assassins. Similarly, the type of person who is bent on pressing home an attack at close quarters with a knife would not, ordinarily, resort to using a clandestinely placed bomb. Assassins have personal preferences and feel comfortable operating in certain ways but not in others. There are some multi-talented assassins, but in terrorist groups there is usually a clear division of labor so that those who are more proficient in some arms will utilize certain weapons to the exclusion of others. With terroristic as well as criminal groups, a definite pattern or *modus operandi* is established over a long period and this constitutes—and is sometimes intended to constitute—virtually a signature or identification of the assassin and his group. These indicators are very important to the intelligence analysts, and knowledge of them forms an important element of the protective system that is being set up where a protracted terrorist campaign is launched at the target figure and his associates. In the matter of weaponry, a number of useful assumptions can be made to facilitate the protective planning functions. It can be assumed, nowadays, that those seeking to assassinate someone will have the means to acquire whatever may be necessary to do the job.[37] It is the assessment of precisely what is required that marks out the professional from the amateur or purely opportunistic assassin. Only the most amateur of assassins would undertake the job with inadequate preparation or without proper means, and those who are merely opportunistic will generally have the means at their disposal to effect their purpose if the opportunity presents itself. The professional will, however, choose his weaponry with the greatest of care, paying proper attention to range, penetration and stopping power,[38] or, in the case of explosives, timing and size of charge.

It should always be remembered that the assassin is only human. Most assassinations fail as a result of human error of some sort, whether alone or in combination with equipment or other circumstantial failure. Sometimes this error will be the result of a psychological or emotional factor disturbing the equilibrium of the assassin at a crucial moment,[39] while at other times it will be the result of a mistake or miscalculation, or inadequate abilities displayed in pressing home the attack. A nervous assassin who is intent on assuring his own escape might well be unable to get sufficiently close to his subject to ensure success. A sentimental assassin might hesitate for that vital fraction of a second to allow an innocent third party to leave the target area.[40] Similarly, nervousness may lead to a loss of concentration or alternatively a deflection of aim that will frustrate the assassin's purpose. Sentimentality can have a similar effect. Where time and place are vital for success, these human failings will frustrate the most careful planning. Protective measures should be designed with these human fallibilities in mind. Anything that is likely to raise the anxiety levels of the assassin and to produce nervousness or lack of concentration in him is a desirable security feature. Such features should, ideally, act upon the mind of the assassin at the moment he is in greatest need of calm and detachment. Security systems should always be designed with the intention of stretching human capacity to the maximum, for example, by keeping the assassin out of range or by moving the protected subject so quickly that it is difficult for the assassin to focus upon him long enough to be able to effect his purpose. The good security system is one which confuses the attacker and reduces to an unacceptable minimum the time he has for calculating his options and taking action.

Assassinations of prominent public figures seem to be affected by cyclical factors.[41] At times, throughout the world, there is a rash of assassination attempts apparently unrelated to each other. On deeper examination, there appears to be a connecting factor which is not immediately apparent from a more superficial examination of the matter. Waves of assassinations do not occur spontaneously. There is a little known contagion factor involved in these cases. At times, there will be an obvious connection between the events; for example, where a systematic terrorist campaign is in progress to intimidate a large class of persons associated in some way politically, ideologically or economically. In other cases, the rash of assassinations will appear to spread across the face of the globe in a somewhat random manner connected only by the association of time rather than geographic space. We are living in an age of extraordinary potency in the area of mass communications. Assassinations are news, especially if the victim is an important public figure. Events that are occurring in one part of the world are now capable of being rapidly made known to persons in another. The message of fear contained in assassination is quickly transmitted elsewhere. It is true "Propaganda of the Deed."[42] From the terroristic perspective, what is seen to work in one area is rapidly followed by imitation in another where the factors seem to suggest that such "technology transfer" is possible or desirable. The true dynamics and extent of the contagion factor are still a matter of controversy and discussion, but the effect of the mass media upon the class of persons likely to commit assassinations cannot be disregarded in any security planning. Certainly there is persuasive evidence that the mentally disturbed are critically influenced by the prospects of publicity.[43] There is no need, here, to discuss in detail the phenomenon of contagion in relation to the potentialities of the various types of mass media. Certain types of publicity generate ideas while others are a stimulus to action. From the perspective of those who are engaged in security planning, it is simply a factor that must be taken into account. It cannot be changed by them, and its influences must be carefully assessed and allowed for in any of the measures designed to ensure the safety of individual protectees. Once the cycle is effectively broken, the harmful effects of publicity are noticeably diminished.

Anti-assassination measures, like all those concerned with security generally, can be divided into "hard" measures and "soft" measures. Among the "soft" measures will be those that are designed to affect, in an indirect fashion, the prospects of an individual surviving a planned assassination upon his person. Prominent among such measures are those concerned with the identification of potential assailants. Something in the nature of a profile of the prospective assassin has to be built up in order to aid those who are engaged in protecting the person of the individual under actual operational conditions. The assassin is unknown, but not unknowable. They need to know *who* they must look for, *what signs* are likely to indicate danger of assassination, and *what sort* of an attempt is likely to occur. It is generally much easier to identify, visually, those who are likely to engage in a direct confrontation-type assault, such as that involved in an attack with a firearm or other weapon at close range, than it is to identify a bomb-setter or a poisoner. Those who operate clandestinely give little indication of their presence and intentions even in the execution phase. *It is never a good policy to rely overmuch upon the use of profiles in identifying potential attackers.*[44] Nevertheless, they are useful, *within their limits,*and the identification of potential assailants through proper intelligence analysis should become an ordinary part of the security planning service.[45] It is important to remember that assassins will not, generally, be distinguished from the ordinary mass of people either by dress, by physical characteristics, by attitudes, or by their behavior until, with regard to this latter, the very moment of launching their attack. Many of the most ordinary looking people harbor the most deadly intent. The "ordinariness" of the assassin is an essential part of his own protective cover and, in the case of professional assassins, this is developed to a high degree. The emergence of the new breed of women terrorists poses its own problems of profiling and identification. Women are prominent in many terrorist groups and take the role of assassin with ease.[46] Women were responsible for two attempts on the life of the President of the United States in 1975.

Many of those undertaking assassination will be persons who suffer from a certain mental imbalance in some degree or another.[47] This is not to say that all assassins are necessarily suffering from any pronounced identifiable mental disease, but rather that, as a rule, their overall personality is strongly affected by some bias or instability produced by psychological or other factors that mark them out from the ordinary run of human individuals. Assassination, even to the strongly motivated, does not come easily. The number of persons who are *natural* predators or killers is comparatively small. Some persons can be trained to kill or can train themselves to kill, while still others would find it impossible to kill under any circumstances.[48] The number of "natural" killers is, fortunately, somewhat small, and this is a factor that must be taken into account in all security planning. The number of these who would, or could, undertake assassination is smaller still. Those who have the ability to kill cold-bloodedly and efficiently, and undertake the necessary training for this dedication, obviously constitute the most serious threat.[49] In the operational performance of all others there will be serious defects that will assist materially in the anti-assassination measures prepared against them. On the assumption, then, that all potential killers are suffering to some degree from a mental imbalance of the kind indicated, it becomes necesary, for security purposes, to differentiate between potential assassins and those with no harmful intent, by reference to some more useful criterion than their state of mind or constitutional condition. This may be useful as a guide, but it is not determinative. It is their motivation, their reasons for undertaking the assassination, that is, perhaps, the most revealing and useful factor for offering a classification of them. These motives, in all their factual richness, are often extremely diverse, but they can be reduced for the purposes of analytical simplicity to encompass those who:

(1) *Undertake assassination for motives of revenge.* This may

be personal or impersonal. The individual assassin may feel himself directly and personally wronged by the individual whose life he will attempt to take,[50] or he might imagine himself to be acting on behalf of a larger class of persons or as a type of "Robin Hood" figure.[51] An example of such an assassination is that of Rafael Trujillo, the Dominican Dictator killed by army officers in 1961.

(2) *Kill strictly for purpose of gain.* This gain may be material or ideological, but the death of the victim is always seen as being in the nature of a real gain for the individual undertaking the assassination or for society as a whole. Professionals generally kill only for material gain; they are, in effect, mercenaries.[52]

(3) *Assassinate in order to affect the balance of power.* This, once more, is a type of killing for gain and it, too, may be for the sense of personal power deriving from the removal of the individual assassinated or, more usually, to affect the balance of power in a wider sense in the interest of some group or society as a whole. The latter is exemplified by the killing, in 1965, of Malcolm X, the American Black Nationalist leader.

Generally speaking, those who kill for a power motive will be undertaking such an assassination for others, either as mercenaries or through ideological commitment, rather than for their own power purposes.

In order that a meaningful identification of potential assailants can take place, a thorough social analysis must be undertaken to determine, so far as possible, whether there exist revolutionary, economic, ideological, or personal causes in sufficient strength to regard any particular person as being a natural target for a potential assassination attempt. A person who is a symbol, who is highly controversial, who has real power or influence, and whose removal should change the course of events in an important way, is an obvious target for assassination.[53] While it is often easy to identify, with hindsight, these factors, it is rarely possible to do more than make a rough estimate of the prospects with the information that is generally available to those entrusted with providing a measure of protection against assassination. *Such speculative exercises should never be made a substitute for hard information.* They are, nevertheless, a useful supplementary device in increasing or decreasing the measures of protection that can be given to particular individuals.

By and large, ideological assassins will be concerned primarily with the elimination of public figures, usually political figures, who are seen to stand in the way of the advancement of their cause. Nevertheless, where the premises of the ideology itself extend to the destruction of a competing ideology such as an attack upon capitalism, generally a class of persons may be seen as symbolic or representative of the opposition in such a way as to mark them out quite impersonally as targets for assassination. Persons who are seen as standing in the way of these objectives as individuals may become potential targets and are then to be ranked for the purposes of assessment of their prospects of assassination upon grounds related to their own relative importance to these objectives rather than by reference to purely ideological considerations. The degree to which those on some lesser plane of political, economic, or other social activity stand in peril from the assassin of ideological persuasion is measured by the intensity of action undertaken by the group or groups to which the ideological assassins belong. Generally speaking, those on a lower executive level, or those who are not prominently in the public eye, will only stand in danger from ideological assassins where there is a general, highly intense campaign against the organizations of which they are representative or the interests with which they might be identified.[54] The risk of assassination at the lower executive levels is increased as the campaign becomes more generalized. If the ideological target is "American business," all American businessmen are potential targets.

Assassination can be either the work of individuals acting strictly alone or in concert with others. As a rule, assassins who work strictly alone in both the planning and execution phases will fall into the seriously mentally disturbed category. Most lone assassins of heads of state fall into this class. Those who merely perform the actual act of execution alone will generally rely upon certain support systems and will have the benefit of advance planning undertaken by others. This is almost invariably the case where the professional, mercenary assassin is concerned. Ideological assassins, whatever their degree of expertise, will invariably work in groups even though the actual act of assassination is entrusted to one single individual.[55] The assassination can, therefore, be characterized by reference to the degree of planning among those involved that goes into the act. In the main, therefore, assassination will be seen to have a covert, conspiratorial character that is somewhat like an iceberg, with the greater part of it concealed from view with only the execution phase of the activity being exposed to the reactive measures that can be taken against it. Even the best intelligence system is unlikely to produce much prior information about the lone assassin, although mentally disturbed individuals will often have issued threats or warnings that should always be thoroughly investigated.[56]

Good security against assassination is largely a matter of foresight. It is the art of having available the maximum amount of protection where it will be most effective against the anticipated threat. The protection must be of the right type for the job. No amount of protective armor will be effective against a lethal dose of poison ingested by the victim in the course of a meal. The right "hardware" can be very important, but it can be utterly useless if the human element is inadequate. The same basic rules apply to those designing protective measures as to those who are encompassing the downfall of the victim. The basic rule should be: *KEEP IT SIMPLE.* Murphy's Law operates in this as in so many other areas of life: if anything *can* go wrong, it *will* go wrong. Security systems that are complicated, particularly those where there is a great deal of room for human error, almost invariably go wrong. The risk of error, particularly in the matter of communications, should be reduced to a minimum.[57] Response time is of the essence and seconds often make the difference between life and death. Every assassination, like every other terroristic act, has a *planning and preparation phase,* an *execution phase,* and an *aftermath.* Certain measures will be designed specifically to act upon the terrorist and his associates in the planning and preparation stage. This is the safest stage for the potential victim, because if the attempt can be frustrated before he is involved in the actual violence, he is unlikely to be harmed in any way by it. Indeed, ideally, he should be unaware that he has been exposed to danger. Once the assassination has entered upon its execution phase, the only protection that can be afforded the individual is by reference to "hardware," such as protective clothing, protective vehicles, shields, the protection that can be afforded by the reaction of human beings, or accidental circumstances. A well-directed assassination attempt is difficult to frustrate once it has begun. It is a sobering thought that, statistically, about one in every two assassination attempts are successful.[58] The good security system seeks to match the type and quality of the protective arrangements to the nature and intensity of the perceived threat. On balance, with assassination, the advantage lies with the attacker. Protective arrangements are largely a matter of whittling down that advantage to manageable proportions.

NOTES

1. *Charles XII of Sweden* (New York: Weybright and Talley, 1968), p. 384.
2. See, for example, *Assassination and Political Violence: A Staff Report to the National Commission on the Causes and Prevention of Violence* (Washington, D.C.: U.S. Government Printing Office, 1969), pp. 1-2, "Problems of Definition."
3. Ibid. pp. 67-73.
4. For example, the Random House Dictionary, unabridged edition, gives: "(1) to kill suddenly or secretively; murder premeditately and treacherously, (2) to destroy or denigrate treacherously and viciously."
5. On this extraordinary sect, see Steven Runciman, *A History of the Crusades* (Cambridge, England: University Press, 1962), vol. 2, pp. 119 et seq.
6. It is worth commenting that this operation that required tunnelling to an exact spot under the roadway, the conveyance of a large quantity of high explosives, and a certain precision in its detonation was greatly facilitated by the Prime Minister's unfailing regularity of habits.
7. The M'Naghten case was a classic example of the lone, mentally disturbed individual pursuing the goal of assassination quite determinedly despite the delusional web in which the perpetrator had become enmeshed. M'Naghten's preparations were methodical and effective and only his error in identification of the target saved the real victim from the intended harm. For an interesting perspective, see Richard Moran, "Awaiting the Crown's Pleasure," 15 *Criminology,* no. 1, May, 1977, pp. 7-26.
8. Thus M. Barthou, the French Foreign Minister who was shot during the assassination of King Alexander in 1934, can be said to have been an accidental victim although there is some evidence that his death was not unwelcome to those who were behind the perpetrators. He died, largely as a result of not receiving medical aid promptly enough, but he was not the real target.

9. On this, see Edward Hyams, *Terrorists and Terrorism* (New York: St. Martin's Press, 1974), p. 121.

10. These will only be apparent when a close range assault is contemplated and are difficult to distinguish from ordinary crowd movements at a distance. The seconds covering the presentation of the weapon are vital and recognition is greatly aided by watching films and simulated situations.

11. *Assassination and Political Violence: A Staff Report to the National Commission on the Causes and Prevention of Violence,* pp. 57-58.

12. Sometimes unexpected or unlooked for opportunity will present itself, but advantage can only be taken of it if the assassin is in place and ready to act. This necessarily requires a regular and systematic seeking of the opportunity.

13. For a good example of what is involved, see the description of the preparations for the killing of Thomas E. Dewey by organized crime figures in *Murder, Inc.* by Burton B. Turkus and Sid Feder (New York: Bantam Books, 1972), chapter 6.

14. See, for example, the case of Demetrio Tsafendas, who in 1966 assassinated Dr. Hendrick Vervoerd, Prime Minister of South Africa.

15. The prospective target of assassination must have a certain *perceived importance.* The victim must have some *special significance* for those desiring his death. Someone must care enough to do the job. The historical context must be right. Opportunity must exist for the type of message the assassination is intended to convey.

16. *Assassination and Political Violence: A Staff Report to the National Commission on the Causes and Prevention of Violence,* pp. 70-91.

17. Consider, for example, the assassination of President Salvador Allende of Chile. Had he survived the coup, he would have constituted a serious obstacle to the designs of those seeking to change the existing political situation in Chile.

18. See Michael Amrine, *This Awesome Challenge* (New York: G.P. Putnam's Sons, 1964), p. 14. President Johnson was concerned lest the death of President Kennedy had been part of a worldwide conspiracy of which he too was a potential victim.

19. This is most particularly the case where dictators and other absolute rulers are concerned. Any system that distributes power militates against assassination for this reason.
20. The more persons involved in subversive, illicit activity of this sort, the more difficult it is to keep it secret. Some assassinations have been carried out by a comparatively large number of persons, but these have generally been in situations amounting to a coup d'etat.
21. "... [it] doesn't bother me, not one bit. This is my job. It is my business. I shoot people and that's it. I never think in terms of morality, although that may be hard for a lot of people to believe. I know the difference between right and wrong. By most standards of morality what I do would be considered wrong. But this doesn't bother me." Joey with Dave Fisher, *Killer* (Chicago, Ill: Playboy Press, 1973), p. 74. This book, incidentally, is a mine of information on all matters relating to the professional killer and is deserving of the closest study. See, too, John Kidner, *Crimaldi: Contract Killer* (Washington, D.C.: Acropolis Books, 1976).
22. On the effects of combat stress, which have many analogies to what is being discussed here, see S.L.A. Marshall, *The Soldier's Load and the Mobility of a Nation* (Washington, D.C.: Combat Forces Press, 1950).
23. Such sentiments are not always unjustified. Many "palace revolts" begin with a subversion of those whose duty it is to provide protection. In many cases, the loyalty of those closest to the target figure can be purchased at a price and an analysis of many revolutionary situations leads to a certain appreciation of the apprehensions of those enjoying this doubtful protection. Such cases have occurred, not infrequently, in organized crime in the United States.
24. There is occasionally an unhealthy rivalry between the analyst and the field agent. The latter is somewhat contemptuous of the former as being a "desk warrior" and this attitude id heartily reciprocated by those who tend to regard their own intellectual capacities as being of a superior order. Harmony and a close working relationship are essential to the effective functioning of the system and thought should be given to the various ways of promoting this.

25. It is pertinent to observe that those who have been kidnapped will often have the opportunity of learning, at first hand, how thoroughly the task of collecting pertinent information has been carried out by the perpetrators; those who are assassinated have no such hindsight granted to them.

26. This is particularly the case with what has become known as psycholinguistics. This is an area in which ordinary semanticists must tread warily. It is reported that Dr. (now Senator) S.I. Hayakawa, called in by the Oakland Tribune to analyze the first SLA communique, pronounced it the work of "a high-grade intellect." David Boulton, *The Making of Tania Hearst* (London: New English Library, 1975), p. 59.

27. Game theory can be very helpful in this. For this applied to kidnapping see Reinhard Selten, *Hostage-Taking: Problems of Prevention and Control* (Montreal: International Center for Comparative Criminology, 1976), pp. 195-218.

28. Sometimes the course of history is altered by a miscalculation of a fraction of a second. On September 8, 1961, a huge hole was blown in the road at Pont-Sur-Seine, France, just after the car carrying Charles De Gaulle had passed.

29. An extraordinary attempt was made on the life of Adolph Hitler on November 8, 1939. After months of work, an explosive device was secreted in a pillar above and behind the rostrum where Hitler was to speak in a Munich restaurant. A mere 13 minutes after the Fuehrer had left the hall the device exploded, killing eight and wounding sixty.

30. "In the shadows behind the closed shutters above a shop selling women's underwear crouched a man. He lay full-length on a cupboard, holding a Mauser repeater rifle. His eye was close to the sight. From his perch, where no one could see him from the street, he saw General De Gaulle, standing erect in his car, come into his line of vision. He followed the General's head with his foresight. His finger was on the trigger. His target was only 14 feet away—impossible to miss. It remained in his line of fire for four seconds. Then the General's head disappeared. The man had not pressed the trigger." Pierre Demaret and Chris-

tian Plume, *Target De Gaulle* (New York: Dial Press, 1975), p. 112. This book is a mine of information on assassination.

31. Premeditation and planning are usually revealed by the acquisition of a weapon, or its being carried, unaccustomedly, in the expectation of an opportunity presenting itself. Assassination is never the result of a chance encounter, It is a combination of means and opportunity, and the means do not come to hand without preparation.

32. There are many deaths of public figures in unexplained circumstances. It has recently been reported that: "What 'Stone' [a top-level Soviet defector] revealed in the months ahead was staggering. He told how he had heard from the head of the Northern-European section of the KGB that the Soviets had planned to kill a leader of an opposition party in his area. Since Hugh Gaitskell, Harold Wilson's rival in Britain's Labor Party, was the only opposition leader to die at this time, and he died of a very rare virus infection, counterintelligence officers in the CIA suspected that the Soviets had done away with Gaitskell to promote Harold Wilson, but the facts never could be established." *New York,* February, 1978, p. 31. Covert assassinations are carried out where the principal value of the operation is in the successful elimination of the target figure, not in the attendant publicity.

33. Of British Ambassador to Ireland, Christopher Ewart-Biggs, it has been said: "The guy was blown up by a land mine—a land mine, for God's sake. You don't walk up to somebody's car and just stick a land mine under it, you plant the damned thing. As I understand it, it was stuck in a culvert under the road and then detonated electronically from behind some bushes a few hundred yards away. My question is: Why didn't the Ambassador go some other way? Why wasn't his route varied? Where were his security people?" Jim Kelly, *Sun Magazine,* August 29, 1976, p. 21.

34. See, for example, the assassination of King Alexander of Yugoslavia in Marseilles, October 9, 1934. The motivation was very complicated, involving questions of both national and international politics. The assassin was shot and killed and his accomplices arrested. Viewed in the wider context, the goals were broadly achieved.

35. *Murder, Inc.,* Burton B. Turkas and Sid Federa (New York: Bantam Books, 1972).

36. Most instructive is the assassination in 1961 of the Prime Minister of the Republic of the Congo, Patrice Lumumba. The circumstances surrounding his death have never been precisely clarified despite a United Nations inquiry and the attentions of the United States Senate Intelligence Committee. The assassination was most successful and clearly had the desired political effect.

37. Firearms are rarely difficult to acquire, even where strict controls are in force. The professional assassin rarely takes the risk of transporting weapons or using those that might be traced to him. An expert has testified: "Any of us who know a little something about it—and anyone could learn it—can go to the drug store, a hardware store and a filling station and make the best bomb you ever saw." William K. Byrd, *Control of Explosives,* Hearings before the Subcommittee to Investigate the Administration of the Internal Security Act and Other Internal Security Laws of the Committee on the Judiciary of the United States Senate. (Washington, D.C.: U.S. Government Printing Office, 1976), p. 198.

38. The West German terrorists have been particularly thorough in this regard, choosing automatic weapons singularly well suited for the operations undertaken. Protective armor and other defensive techniques must be carefully matched to such developments.

39. Fear not only causes the hands to shake and palms to sweat, thereby spoiling aim, but is also sometimes responsible for errors like leaving the safety catch on or not having a bullet in the chamber. Freudian psychoanalysts would offer other equally pertinent explanations.

40. Grand Duke Sergei, later assassinated, survived an attempt on his life in 1905 because his two anarchist assassins could not go through with their bombing because he was accompanied on the occasion by his wife and two young nephews.

41. A veritable fever swept across the world during the final quarter of the last century and before the outbreak of the First World War. Many of these killings were unrelated save by reference to the vast groundswell of history. Others, like the assassination of Archduke Franz Ferdinand

at Sarajevo were part of more sinister, international conspiracies designed to alter the world balance of power.

42. This is a phrase coined by the French Socialist Paul Brousse in 1878 and it has since become a creed of all anarchists and their ideological confreres.

43. The case of David Berkowitz, the so-called "Son of Sam," is worthy of careful study in this regard. It is evident that the attendant publicity was of the greatest importance to him, and it played a large part in the acting out of his fantasies.

44. The widely accepted criteria for the identification of presidential assassins would have excluded Lynette Fromme and Sarah Jane Moore.

45. On this, generally, see *Assassinations and Political Violence: A Staff Report to the National Commission on the Causes and Prevention of Violence*, p. 95. "Our analysis must distinguish between possible assassins and potential assassins."

46. See, for example, "A New Breed: The Female Assassins," *Argosy* Special, 1976, pp. 21-29.

47. This is a very complicated matter. For an excellent example of a particular case, see Robert Blair Kaiser, *R.F.K. Must Die!* (New York: E.P. Dutton, 1970), especially chapter 19.

48. On this, see the work of Samuel L.A. Marshall, particularly *Men Against Fire* (New York: Apollo, 1961). "Joey" writes: "A lot of people will point a gun at you, but they haven't got the courage to pull the trigger. It's as simple as that. I would give you odds on almost anybody you name that, if I put a gun in his hand, he would not pull the trigger." *Murder, Inc.,* at page 75.

49. Such killers are not infrequently attracted to the ranks of organized terrorists. Among many examples may be mentioned the notorious "Carlos." For an interesting thumbnail sketch, see Ovid Demaris, "Carlos: The Most Dangerous Man in the World," *New York,* November 7, 1977, p. 35.

50. This seems to have been the case of the assassin of King Faisal of Saudi Arabia, who in 1975 put two bullets in his uncle's head seemingly to avenge a brother killed by Saudi police nine years earlier.

51. Thus, the convicted assassin of Pancho Villa declared:

"I'm not a murderer. I rid humanity of a monster."

52. Considerable mystery still surrounds the death in 1961 of Patrice Lumumba, Premier of the Congo. A U.N. inquiry suggests he was killed by Belgian mercenaries. The 1975 U.S. Senate Intelligence Committee report suggests United States implication.

53. "[No] symbol in the United States is more potent than the presidency." *Assassinations and Political Violence: A Staff Report to the National Commission on Causes and Prevention of Violence,* p. 102.

54. It has been said that: ". . . [if] you terrorize the base of the Establishment, you deliver a telling blow at the System's main body perhaps more surely and swiftly than if you concentrate on its top reaches." Albert Parry, *Terrorism From Robespierre to Arafat* (New York: Vanguard Press, 1976), p. 523.

55. The assassin of Mahatma Ghandi, Nathuram Godse, took sole responsibility for the assassination and fired the fatal shots. He was, however, part of a conspiracy of seven persons who had planned the killing for some time and who had made an unsuccessful attempt 10 days earlier.

56. It is very important that these investigations and their results be capable of rapid retrieval. It is equally important not to lose sight of those who make threats of this kind, for, in the case of many assassinations, the perpetrator is seen to be linked with a past threat or a past attempt.

57. Given the importance of communications, on both sides, to the success or failure of the terrorist enterprise, some considerable thought and training should be given in this area. It should be assumed that in any serious attack, an attempt will be made to interfere with or interrupt the primary communications system. Hand and voice signals are limited in range by considerations of line of sight and distance. A sudden loss of communication causes confusion and disorientation. The use of the police whistle is a simple and effective emergency means of communication. It is unwise to rely totally on two-way radios or landlines.

58. See *Assassination and Political Violence: A Staff Report to the National Commission on the Causes and Prevention of Violence,* p. 117.

Kidnapping

"I must say, reciting this experience, this story, is quite painful to me even now because both my wife and I went through quite a lot during those 3½ days, and you can't have anything like that happen to you without it making some mark, and it has made a rather lasting mark, I think."

Ambassador C. Burke Elbrick[1]

Kidnapping is an age-old, well-tried criminal technique that has been refined and adapted in modern times for terroristic purposes. It poses a particularly severe threat to public figures and others in many parts of the world today. *Kidnapping may be defined as the violent or non-violent seizure of control and custody of another human being and his subsequent detention in a clandestine place for the purpose of obtaining a ransom or something of value from those who are interested in the safety and well-being of the victim.* There are a number of indispensable elements that serve to distinguish this crime from others of a similar nature.[2] The prime object of the crime is extortion through the coercion of those persons interested in the life and safety of the victim who is in the power of the kidnappers. It is evident that kidnapping can only be successful if there are persons interested in the life and safety of the victim and who are prepared to accede to the demands of those having seized control and custody of his person. If there is literally nobody interested in the victim or if the victim's interests are subordinated to a wider social interest, then the whole purpose of the crime is defeated. The victim's value to the kidnapper lies in the reaction of society in general and the intimates of the victim in particular. The crime is thus designed to appeal to the natural humanity of persons in civilized societies and constitutes a severe threat to those whose susceptibilities make them a natural prey of those who would hold them for ransom. *The essence of the crime is extortion;* and the kidnapper threatens to destroy the interest over which he has control, namely the human life, just as the blackmailer threatens to expose his victim or to destroy his reputation unless his demands are met. Kidnapping is a trial of strength with a helpless human being caught in the middle.

Kidnapping is the clandestine crime *par excellence.* The victim must be taken to, and forcibly kept in, a secret location. He will, ideally, be taken there as secretively as possible. It is the inability of the authorities to find this location that constitutes at one and the same time the kidnapper's power over the victim and society in general, and his shield against any countermeasures that might be taken against him. The whole dynamic of the crime turns upon this element of secrecy; without it, the crime becomes something entirely different.[3] It is of the utmost importance to the kidnapper to maintain the secrecy of his operations and, in particular, the place where he has detained the victim. All his activities are, therefore, tinged with the utmost secrecy and are designed to reveal as little as possible of the identity of those involved in the operation, their strength, and, in particular, their location.

While it is possible to envisage the case of the lone kidnapper and, indeed, some kidnappings have been carried out by individuals working without any cooperation from others, kidnapping is almost invariably a group endeavor. Terrorist kidnappings, and political kidnappings in particular, are mainly well-organized group activities in which a considerable division of labor has been undertaken in the interests of the operation. As in the case of assassination, different people will have different degrees of involvement; but as a kidnapping is a more protracted process in the execution phase, more people will generally come into contact with the victim or with the authorities during the course of the operation. Some will be involved in the actual seizure, others will be custodians, some will have communications roles, while yet others will be almost totally insulated from the operation and will have a strictly directive role.

The actual seizure of control and custody of the individual may or may not be of a violent nature. In many kidnappings, particularly those where the victim realizes what is afoot, there will be a need for force, or the threat of force, on the part of those who are trying to carry off the victim.[4] In other cases, the victim will be tricked into going with the kidnappers or will be taken by means of a ruse or in such a way that effective resistance is suppressed. The victim is often a child quite unable to put up any real resistance at all. The fact that the victim may cooperate with the kidnapper to some extent in surrendering to him does not change the character of the crime. What is involved here is the creation of massive fear, through suggestion or otherwise, by the kidnapper so as to overcome the will of the victim. The victim is put in fear throughout the duration of the crime by the constant threat held over his life by the kidnapper. That fear will be intensified in a practical way whenever the kidnapper sees the need to reinforce his demands.

Kidnapping is distinguished from abduction, to which it is closely related, by reason of the intrinsic value the victim has for the purposes of effecting an exchange for something else that the kidnapper desires. In the case of pure abduction, what the abductor desires is permanent control and custody of the victim and nothing else.[5] The abductor is not desirous of exchanging the victim for anything else of value. Most abductions are of a family nature or involve other relationships of an intimate kind. In the case of a true kidnapping, the victim is of incidental value as such, and the kidnapper merely retains control and custody of him until such time as he is able to exchange the victim for what he really desires.

Like assassination, kidnapping is a deliberate and premeditated crime. While it is possible to conceive of a case of mistaken identity in which the wrong victim is taken, there can be no such thing as an accidental kidnapping. Kidnappings need to be carefully planned and rarely take place on the spur of the moment. In most cases, an even higher degree of selectivity operates in the case of kidnapping than in the case of assassination. Kidnap victims are deliberately chosen because of their *assumed* value to those who will try to ransom them. Kidnap victims are chosen, too, because they are assumed to have a high exchange value, a value commensurate at least with that of the object which the kidnapper desires in exchange. This is also an important feature distinguishing kidnapping from hostage taking where the victims may be taken and held for ransom in a much more indiscriminate fashion. From a security perspective, too, this is an important feature because this feature of selectivity tends to point to prospective victims and the need for special protective measures in their case.

While kidnapping is, generally speaking, much more difficult to carry out than assassination, it is, from a terrorist perspective, more productive in many ways than the simple elimination of the victim. Kidnapping, particularly if it is engaged in systematically over a long period, is a great fear-producing activity. It leads to a great deal of insecurity, generally, and casts considerable doubt upon the abilities of law enforcement to provide effective protection to the populace. Even those who stand little threat of direct victimization are intimidated by it and sense the overall climate of insecurity. As it generally strikes at a class which is ordinarily very powerful and conscious of its position in society, the apparent powerlessness of the victim, and those who would assist him before this phenomenon, is a striking demonstration of the ability of the perpetrators to defy the authorities. This is particularly well demonstrated where the victim is kept alive and hidden over a long period while the authorities are, through the news media, forced to publish the kidnappers' communiques and evidence of the victim's condition as has been done in many notorious cases; in particular, that involving Herr Hanns-Martin Schleyer in West Germany in 1977. The Patricia Hearst case is illustrative of the same point.

Apart from the complexity of the kidnapping operation itself and the difficult logistics involved in taking a live victim, secreting that victim, and entering into the delicate negotiations for his (or her) exchange, there is a further, human factor which is extremely important in relation to this crime. The kidnapping can extend over a lengthy period from the time of the seizure of the individual until his demise or eventual release. During this time, there develops a complex human interaction between the victim and his captors which is or can be extremely influential in deciding the outcome of the event. Once the actual crime has been set in motion, the potential assassination victim has generally only a split-second in which, personally, to take action which might influence the prospects of his survival. Personal interaction with the assassin is rarely possible or likely to deflect him from his course. The kidnap victim, on the other hand, may have days, weeks, or even months and years, during which his own actions might spell death for him or ensure his prospects of survival or escape. This introduces an entirely novel dimension into any discussion on protective measures, for these must be designed not only with a view to preventing, if possible, the actual transfer of control and custody, but must be directed as well to preserving the life and safety of the individual during the period of his captivity.

An individual selected as a target for assassination can do much to reduce the prospects of harm to his person during the pre-execution phase. Once that execution phase has commenced, however, there is comparatively little that he can then do to ensure his own safety and to frustrate the assassination attempt. Such measures of self-defense as he might take, from a close-quarter attack, will be mostly instinctive, even if he is well trained and prepared for such an eventuality. He must rely for his protection mainly on the efforts of others. With kidnap victims there is much that they can do to avoid being victimized in the first place. But they themselves might well be the only means of their own survival once the kidnapping has actually taken place. From the standpoint of protective services, therefore, the early involvement of potential kidnap victims is essential in order that these aspects of survival receive proper, professional attention. Unlike assassination, kidnapping has this extended execution phase during which the real protection of the victim, by the forces of society is temporarily withdrawn, and the victim is, in effect, cast upon his own resources in order to ensure his survival while efforts are being made to rescue him. The teaching of such survival techniques, or *how to minimize the risk of harm during the execution phase,* should be regarded as an important part of the integral protective effort to provide for the safety and survival of the kidnap victim.[6]

From the point of view of the kidnappers, there are a number of requisites that must be met for a successful kidnapping. There must be, in the first instance, a successful taking of the desired victim. If the victim is injured or killed in the process of seizing control and custody, the whole character of the operation is changed and the basic premise of the kidnapping is frustrated. There is no kidnapping until the victim is effectively reduced into the power of the kidnapper.[7] The objective is not the elimination of the individual but a seizure of him in order that he may be exchanged at some later time. *The victim has to be taken alive and has to be kept alive until such time as he can be effectively exchanged.* To a certain extent, the objective of the kidnappers can be said to coincide with those of the authorities and the friends and relatives of the victim: all are desirous of keeping the victim alive.[8] So far as the kidnappers are concerned, this may well change during the course of the kidnapping according to the contingencies that present themselves. At the start, however, while the prime objective of the kidnappers remains unchanged, the safety of the victim is assured less by material circumstances than by reason of the predominant need of the kidnappers to satisfy those with whom they are dealing that they have a live victim to exchange.[9]

In the second place, the kidnappers must have a suitable, safe haven where the kidnap victim can be kept in reasonably good condition until the time has come to exchange him. The importance of clandestineness cannot be overstressed in this matter. Once the hideout is discovered, the real power of the kidnapper is substantially broken. This may not save the life of the victim, but it destroys the point of the crime or turns it into something else. The effectiveness of the whole operation depends upon the location of the victim not being prematurely discovered by law enforcement so that that location can be invested and captured with the victim alive or dead. So long as the location of the victim remains a secret, the power of the kidnappers remains largely intact and they are able to deal with the authorities and others at arm's-length with the certainty that their bargaining power is unimpaired.

Thirdly, the kidnappers have a real need to establish their own credibility in the eyes of those with whom they are dealing. This is rather less obvious than it might appear at first sight. They have to show, above all else, that they do, indeed, have the victim and that the victim is alive and well at the moment any bargain is contemplated for his release. Nobody wishes to meet demands of any nature only to find that in return the victim is already dead and can only be delivered over in the shape of a corpse.[10] It is not generally too difficult for the kidnappers to show that they have, indeed, seized the victim. There may well be witnesses to the actual act of kidnapping or there may be substantial evidence that persuades the authorities and those interested that the event has indeed taken place. On the other hand, a kidnapping is not self-evident, and there are other plausible explanations for the disappearance of individuals from time to time.[11] The principal difficulties, so far as credibility is concerned, lie in the subsequent events. It is necessary for the kidnappers to evidence, at any point in time at which they are seeking to make a deal, that the victim is *still* alive and still in their possession. This evidence is much more difficult to provide.[12] Even with the aid of modern technological devices such as tape recorders, it is not easy to satisfy these requirements. Video tapes and photographs of the victim reading a newspaper showing a particular headline or date, or indicating in communications his knowledge of an event that has occurred at a particular time, are no guarantee that he is still alive at the time this information is transmitted to the authorities or those who are seeking to bargain for the release of the victim. The real problem for the kidnappers is how they can do more without, in the process, revealing their own whereabouts. Telephone calls can be traced as, indeed, can other means of communication. The constant struggle for the kidnapper is how to maintain his credibility and his own security in a clandestine fashion at the same time.

Fourthly, this is a crime which puts a very serious strain upon communications from the point of view of those who are engaged in it. Not only must they communicate with the authorities in a satisfactory manner which is consistent with their objectives, maintains their security, and establishes their credibility, they also need to communicate among themselves. All this must be done in such a way that it does not expose them to detection and apprehension. Law enforcement and other security forces that do not have, or are not allowed by law to make use of, modern electronic surveillance techniques are at a considerable disadvantage.[13]

Criminal kidnappings and terrorist kidnappings are virtually indistinguishable in their dynamics and modalities. They both make use, essentially, of the same techniques, and sometimes the same personnel, and have broadly the same objectives. Indeed, in the same geographic location, the two types can co-exist, virtually indistinguishable, side-by-side, as witness the case of present-day Italy and Colombia. Both types pose, essentially, the same problems for law enforcement and private security and follow very much the same operational patterns from the point of view of the perpetrators. Although the distinctions, on occasion, may be slight, they are nevertheless important.

In general, criminal kidnappers are interested almost exclusively in money ransoms, and the amount demanded tends to reflect what is assumed to be the "going rate" at any particular time. Kidnapping becomes a business with a definite attention to cost benefit factors.[14] There is little room for sentiment. Nevertheless, due to this preoccupation with the lucrative aspects of kidnapping, the criminal kidnapper tends to be more anxious and impatient and ready to dispose of the victim if it appears unlikely that his demands are going to be satisfied within a reasonably short space in time. Few criminal kidnappers have the material resources to keep any save the most valuable victims for any length of time. There is an important cost benefit factor here from the point of view of the kidnapper which tends to orient his actions. Most criminal kidnappings, particularly in Latin America, are the work of professional gangs; and they are well organized and ruthless. They tend to confuse the situation and act virtually as a smoke screen that is used by terrorists or politically motivated kidnappers. Where kidnapping has long been endemic, it is difficult for even experienced law enforcement officers immediately to distinguish between the two types.[15] In many countries, too, criminal kidnappings are better organized and executed than political kidnappings because they occur with such regularity. The criminal elements have literally made a way of life out of this type of antisocial activity, and they have reduced its elements to a cold efficiency that is superior in many ways to the efforts of the counterforces directed against them.[16] The political kidnapping phenomenon is often comparatively new; and, although carried out with great enthusiasm, its exponents do not have the same degree of experience or organization as their criminal counterparts.

So far as kidnapping is concerned, the security aspects should focus primarily upon prevention. The objective is to avoid the potential victim falling into the hands of the kidnappers at all. It will be readily appreciated that, from the point of view of those who engage in the business of kidnapping—for whatever reason—it is a considerably more difficult task than undertaking assassination or other purely destructive behavior; there is a necessity to take the victim alive and relatively unharmed and, if he is protected, this will demand considerable organization and a large deployment of force. The consequences of this should be clearly understood by those concerned with developing protective responses. The protective measures that can be taken fall into the "hard" class and the "soft" class as previously indicated. The potential kidnap victim will make much greater use of personal bodyguards to avoid being taken because the perpetrators of this crime must also use considerable manpower in order to effect it; they cannot rely on the use of technological devices to place the victim in their control and custody. Technology favors the protective forces in these cases. The *proper use* of alert, constantly present bodyguards is an extremely important protective device; indeed, in many cases, they are indispensable. It is, however, extremely costly, and it is often this factor that causes the victim to be left without protection at crucial moments.[17] There is a great need, in many cases, for a "requirements analysis" that will show exactly what can be done by other means to supplement the purely human force available for the protection of the individual at his residence, at his principal place of business, and while he is en route between the two, as well as such other places as he may be required to visit in a social or professional capacity. *Hardware and defensive systems should always be regarded as a useful supplement to, rather than a substitute for, the human element of protection provided by the specialist bodyguard.* Thus, the home or place of business can be made more difficult to enter through architectural modifications, various screening processes, the use of sensors, canines and proper entrance control; but, in the last resort, it is the human element that will filter out those who would harm the potential target from those with a legitimate purpose in having relations with him.

As much attention must be paid to the system of procedures as to the actual hardware and the personnel themselves. A defective system can clearly cause problems when one is up against a skilled and determined organization. The possibility of the victim's own organization being infiltrated by those who would harm him should always be considered. Such an individual cannot only provide inside information but can also deflect procedures so as to facilitate a kidnapper's purposes. This is of particular importance where the preventive measures are designed to give the target individual a measure of protection while he is en route from his home to his place of business or elsewhere. If the procedures are inherently defective, for example, bodyguards traveling in a separate vehicle from which they could not bring their own weaponry to bear in the case of an ambush,[18] or where they travel in an enclosed vehicle susceptible to selective small arms fire, the target individual is exposed to a considerable risk that is the fault of those who have designed the system rather than that of the individuals engaged in offering the physical protection. The defensive measures taken must always be adapted to the circumstances of the case and must take into account the lifestyle and professional activities of the potential victim in question. Preventive measures must be custom designed in every case. The potential victim must be schooled not to defeat the system developed for his protection.

The so-called "soft" measures are of the utmost importance to the prevention of kidnapping. *Some victims, consciously or unconsciously, make the task of the kidnapper much easier than it need be.* Their lives have an unfailing regularity about them. Such persons leave home at the same time every day and follow exactly the same route to their place of business. They regularly engage, in social activities of an unvarying nature, and they are extremely exposed at certain times in such a way that even relatively casual observation will make possible the development and execution of a kidnapping plan with considerable ease. The individual concerned is rarely able to see or appreciate the degree to which his activities expose him to the possibility of being kidnapped.[19] There is ingrained in many persons an acute resistance to change and unwillingness to give up habits developed over a lifetime. A careful survey needs to be done by a security specialist in order to measure with some exactitude what is needed to break up the pattern of activity so as to interpose a degree of security through randomness. Additionally, when a victim has been selected as a kidnapping prospect, there are certain signs of this indicative to the trained observer. Surveillance will be carried out in order to formulate the necessary plans, and these signs should become apparent to those who are engaged in protecting the target individual. The surveillance itself will often be most professional and unobtrusive and, on that account, very difficult to detect by a busy individual engaged in his normal business and social affairs. The actual execution of the kidnapping may, however, take place in the most bizarre of circumstances. The kidnapper will generally rely upon surprise and overwhelming force. The watchword as far as kidnapping is concerned is: *watch out for the unexpected.*[20]

Once an individual can be reasonably categorized by those providing protective services as a prospective kidnap victim, a number of precautionary measures must immediately go into effect. The most effective measure is for him to be removed altogether from the place where the kidnapping might be carried out or where it would serve a useful purpose. This is the best solution with non-essential executive personnel overseas who are threatened in this way. If this cannot be done, other measures must be taken. It is as well for the physical protection that he is given to be increased as unobtrusively as possible. It should always appear to those who are trying to undertake the kidnapping that the protective ring with which the victim is surrounded is stronger than it is. The "harder" the target, the more difficult it is to hit and the more likely it is that the kidnappers will expose their intentions and preparations. *There is a paramount need for cooperation between the target figure and those whose duty and responsibility it is to protect him.* Without this cooperation, the victim will be critically exposed in a way that will facilitate the kidnapper's objectives. If the victim, for example, eludes his protectors, for whatever reason, then the kidnapper's patience will have been rewarded. The victim must simply avoid placing himself in a position where he can be taken and his bodyguard overwhelmed. The victim must be in some sort of communication with his bodyguards at all times, and they must be in secure communication with each other and their central office.[21]

For many potential kidnap victims, the classic psychological syndrome of denial takes over. They absolutely refuse to accept the prospect of real danger existing in their case and seek to shut out from their minds altogether the unpleasant possibilities of being kidnapped. This ostrich-like attitude is not only unhelpful, but can be the cause of severe trauma in the event of a kidnapping taking place, and may drastically reduce the prospects of survival. It is necessary for all those who live under the threat of kidnapping to prepare themselves sensibly for such an eventuality, as such preparation will measurably enhance their prospects of survival and may, in itself, be an important element in frustrating the kidnapping. Those who face a serious prospect of becoming kidnap victims need at least a certain basic training. *So, also, do their families and friends.* In the event of a kidnapping taking place, the future safety of the individual may depend on little more than his own ability to follow certain basic procedures to ensure his own survival while efforts are being made by others to secure his release.[22] Such training should, ideally, combine his knowledge of preventive measures that can promptly be taken alone or in cooperation with those entrusted with his protection, and measures designed to ensure survival in the event of a successful kidnapping taking place. These measures must be custom-made, taking into account the potential victim's age, sex, physical and mental condition, with due attention being paid, in the sincerest fashion, to his strengths and weaknesses. There is need for specialized psychological counseling of prospective victims and their families. This will not only fortify their mental health and enable them to perform better during the anxious time while the threat persists, but will enhance the prospects of survival if kidnapping takes place.

Perhaps the most serious question with which the kidnap victim is immediately faced is whether to resist, in any way, the attempt made to reduce him into the control and custody of those who are trying to take him. It is very difficult to offer any useful, general guidance on this point as the circumstances of whether resistance is possible or desirable will depend upon a large number of highly variable factors. Factors to be taken into account would include the location of the kidnapping attempt; the size of the force arrayed against the protective screen, and the victim himself; the age, sex, physical condition and situation of the potential victim (for example, a person sitting down, unarmed, is unlikely to be in *any* condition to resist an armed attack upon his person); and the determination with which the attack is pressed home. Persons well able to protect themselves ordinarily are often rendered unable to do so through surprise. It must be borne in mind that the moment of greatest danger for the kidnap victim is the precise instant at which the kidnapper is trying to exercise his power to obtain full control and custody of him. The kidnapper is uncertain of his prospects of success and, as yet, the victim has not acquired the value from him that he will have later on. These uncertainties will transform themselves into danger for the victim. There will be a natural tendency to overreact; and there will be an excessive use of force due, in part, to the flow of adrenaline and, in part, to the inability to gauge with exactitude how much force might be adequate to effect the kidnapper's purpose. Much unnecessary violence is meted out to victims in the excitement of early moments. Sir Geoffrey Jackson, for example, who was hardly surprised, did not resist in any way but was beaten about the head by one of his nervous, young Tupamaro kidnappers.[23] Nevertheless, if the victim is unable to escape at this moment, he may well not have another chance later on. It is a matter of split-second assessment and preparation, a quick eye, and an ability on the part of the victim to marshal all of his resources for whatever might be necessary. That is the secret of the margin between success and failure in this regard. *Resistance should never be offered in the face of overwhelming force.* It is only likely to provoke the kidnapper into a violent reaction and substantially affect the prospects of the victim's eventual survival. The kidnapper may be panicked into killing the victim rather than attempting to take him away. In the final analysis, the matter depends upon an imponderable: how important is it to the kidnapper to take the victim alive?[24]

Nonresistance should not be confused with the taking of appropriate evasive measures, as, for example, the use of defensive driving techniques in the case of an ambush. The real question is whether an individual, bereft of any form of physical protection, should try to run away, break from the hold of his captors, shout for help in a public place,[25] or otherwise seek to avoid allowing himself to be reduced into the control and custody of those who intend to take him away. Carrying personal weapons is largely a matter of choice. But they should only be carried by individuals well trained in their use and with the knowledge that sometimes they may increase rather than reduce the danger to the victim. Again, other, more remote, circumstances might well dictate the choice of the victim. If he knows that his situation is such that he is unlikely to obtain a negotiated release at some later date or is likely, in any event, to be such an obnoxious target to his captors that the prospects of his survival are slim, he may well prefer to take considerable risk in escaping from his captors at the very moment he is taken. Given the right set of circumstances, an initial show of resistance is sometimes extremely effective and can result in escape.[26] Potential victims should be educated to realize that death is not a certainty even in the presence of a man heavily armed with automatic weapons. *Offering resistance will be essentially an individual choice in all cases.* All that can generally be done in advance is to offer practical guidance on the available alternatives.

Once the kidnapping has actually taken place, the emphasis of the security measures shifts to those intended to aid in the continued survival of the kidnapped victim by external means and those designed to secure his release. Any kidnapping resulting in the death of the victim, whether or not ransom is paid, must be regarded as a failure from a security point of view. From the standpoint of those with responsibility for protective services, a successful outcome implies the safe release of the victim and his restoration to society. The eventual release of the victim can be effected by:

(1) *Attrition* - This is where the kidnapper finally releases the victim of his own volition because he decides to discontinue the operation, or because he has been forced to realize that continued control and custody of the victim no longer serve any useful purpose to him. This is what happened, in effect, when the Tupamaros released the British Ambassador to Uruguay, Sir Geoffrey Jackson, after eight months captivity in 1972.[27] This happens generally where the kidnapping is part of a long series of operations, and it is not considered opportune to kill the victim as it might jeopardize future action.

(2) *Force* - The release of the victim can be effected by force only where the location of the victim can be discovered by the law enforcement authorities, and proper and effective steps taken to assault the position in such a way that the kidnappers are unable to dispatch their victim before the rescue is complete. This is always a hazardous prospect,

for if the endeavors of the authorities become known to the kidnappers and they realize that they are on the verge of being apprehended or their position discovered, they may well be forced into killing the victim and abandoning their project.[28] Discovery of a hideout will sometimes turn the affair into a barricaded hostage situation as occurred with Dr. Tiede Herrema, kidnapped in Eire in October 1975 by two IRA members.

(3) *Negotiation* - This is by far the most common means of effecting the release of the victim. The kidnappers will usually make their demands known at some point in time; a process of bargaining takes place, formally or informally, and some sort of transfer for consideration is made to obtain the release of the victim. Most countries will permit, albeit grudgingly, some form of negotiated settlement with the kidnappers. Very occasionally, the victim is able to negotiate his own release as did the Dutch millionaire, Maurits Caransa, kidnapped by a criminal gang in November, 1977.[29]

The principal security problem is to keep the victim alive while each of these possibilities is explored and developed. Experience suggests that most of the kidnap victims who die do so within the first 36 hours of the kidnapping. For a variety of reasons, the prospects for survival seem to increase the longer the captivity can be prolonged. Hence, the importance of taking any disappearance seriously. Many victims have died because of a reluctance to believe that they have been kidnapped.[30]

On the assumption that the kidnapping has taken place and the victim is effectively reduced into the control and custody of the kidnapper, the question becomes one of how best to handle the situation that has arisen. All protective measures should be directed to ensuring the continued safety and well-being of the victim while he remains in control and custody of the kidnapper. Once proven, *the control and custody of the kidnapper, whether he be a common criminal or a terrorist, is an undisputed fact.* There is little point in getting angry or philosophically offended by this circumstance. It is simply a matter, like any other, that must be taken into consideration in securing the rescue of the victim and his restoration to his former position in society. To a large extent, the way the case is handled will depend on where the kidnapping took place. Regardless of the nationality and position of the victim, it is the laws and customs of the location where the kidnapping took place that will govern the matter. The law enforcement authorities of that particular country will act accordingly, and other interested parties, however influential, must tailor their own conduct to these requirements. This can have important consequences. It may be that unofficial intervention—including the intervention of those who would normally be responsible, in a private sense, for the security of the individual—will be not only unwelcome but will not be permitted at all.[31] There may be laws that prevent any sort of dealing or negotiation with the kidnappers. There may be laws which prevent the payment of ransom.[32] There will almost certainly be laws restricting the exercise of certain functions and privileges by foreign citizens.[33] If the demands extend beyond this, for example, the satisfaction of certain political demands, exchange of prisoners, or matters of that sort, the questions raised may well have to be dealt with at a high political level and will be subject to established policy in that regard. While some foreign governments will deal directly with private citizens and organizations on matters of this kind, others will only deal with official government representatives; and protocol must be followed. The first priority is a coordination of all efforts designed to effect the rescue of the victim. Every endeavor must be made to avoid the creation of antagonisms that might delay resolution of the matter and harm the victim.

In the event of the victim being an American citizen kidnapped abroad, coordination among various government agencies will be required. Each of these agencies has its own particular responsibility and can offer invaluable specialized assistance as the matter develops. In the case of money ransom being demanded, and in the event of this being a negotiable item, it will generally be the responsibility of those having a personal interest in the individual's life and safety to make arrangements for obtaining this money ransom. Official participation will generally only extend to the arrangements for its delivery in return for the victim. Conflicts of interest may well arise during the course of the proceedings. For those who are most directly interested in the individual concerned, his safety and return will be of paramount importance. For the forces of public order, while these considerations are no less material, there will be other matters that will have to be taken into consideration and some order of priorities will have to be established. There should be mutual confidence and a clear understanding among all those concerned with trying to bring about the successful resolution of the kidnapping situation. There often develops an understandable impatience on the part of family and loved ones to ensure the safety of the victim at all costs and, occasionally, it is felt that this concern is not shared, at least in sufficient measure, by the public law enforcement authorities. This sometimes leads to private deals and certain "behind the scenes" working which is counter-productive for all concerned and can well lead to the demise of the victim.[34] Such feelings, though understandable, can be deadly. There should be no misunderstandings regarding these matters that are likely to put in jeopardy the law enforcement endeavors.

In foreign countries, particularly, it is unwise and unhelpful to make enemies of local law enforcement authorities. Sometimes, in the case of prominent individuals, there are pressures brought to bear on the public authorities, and independent steps are taken to try to resolve the matter by extra-official means that may or may not be successful. The more important the victim, the higher the level of responsibility at which the various policy and operational decisions will have to be taken. The more important the victim, too, the more value he will have in the eyes of those who have kidnapped him. This will further complicate the prospects of his safe release. Cooperation, not interference, is called for from those who wish to show their concern.

The actual mechanics of the negotiation are often very complicated. The involved nature of these is designed, in part, to protect the kidnappers from detection and apprehension. There have been cases where the victim has been able to negotiate his own release. More usually, the victim will be almost entirely dependent upon the efforts of those working for his release from outside. *The most important feature is communication.* There is an understandable reluctance on the part of the kidnappers to engage in any form of communication that is likely to imperil their own security or reveal themselves or their hideout. Communications are often very involved, indirect, and extremely frustrating. The problem for both sides is that the ordinary trust that is involved in normal business relations is, in the nature of things, quite absent. The two parties are negotiating with each other in a feeling of mutual apprehension and distrust that is not conducive to good bargaining. Nevertheless, both have an asset that the other wants, and every endeavor should be made to bargain in a way that is likely to be productive of the eventual safe release of the victim. Nothing should be done that might raise the levels of anxiety and mistrust of the kidnappers.

Whenever the demands are so extreme that they cannot possibly be met, every opportunity should be taken to offer acceptable alternatives. Almost invariably, the circumstances are such that the kidnappers can be persuaded to take something less than the extreme demands which they have advanced at the outset.[35] This is particularly the case where a money ransom is concerned. Very often, the demand will have been pitched absurdly high so as to create a more favorable bargaining position. Sometimes the person with the real power to do what the kidnapper requires is not the victim seized but is the person from whom satisfaction is demanded. In other words, a close relative or someone for whom that person has considerable regard is the victim seized by the kidnapper, while the person upon whom the pressure is brought to bear is, in a sense, the ulterior victim. There are many who would take a hard line about their own fate yet would be unwilling, for example, to sacrifice a favorite son. This factor, too, will dictate the course of bargaining. In many of these situations, third parties are brought into the matter either as avenues of communication or as persons who can assist in the resolution of the matter. Some may be genuine intermediaries, having some sort of access to the kidnappers, while others will have only a minor connection with the case by way of information or special skills. Some of these persons are clearly charlatans or are trying to profit from the anguish of those concerned. Others are genuinely helpful and have an important role to play. It is an important responsibility of those who are engaged in the protective aspects of the matter to be able to distinguish between the two. Again, the fullest cooperation with the public agencies concerned is imperative.[36]

The aftermath of any kidnapping, whatever the outcome, is invariably traumatic. The victim, if he is released, will have suffered a very serious experience and will often require medical and psychological treatment over an extended period. His whole lifestyle and activities will have suffered a considerable change, and this is something that requires serious professional attention. He may be so severely incapacitated that he is no longer functional in his former capacity. A great deal of individual and family counseling may be necessary to allay fears and counter suppressed effects of the experience. Perhaps the greatest fear of those living under a continuing threat is that it might happen again, if not to the victim then to someone else closely connected with him. Steps should wherever possible, be taken to remove the victim from a place or position where he or his loved ones might suffer further harm.

Perhaps the most important protective measure that can be taken before a kidnapping actually occurs is for the victim and his family, and those concerned with him in any way, to *keep a low profile.* This is particularly important in those countries where kidnapping has become virtually endemic. Any publicity, particularly in the mass media sources, such as television, glossy magazines, and gossip columns, is likely to provide details on the victim's background, habits, and lifestyle that, if they do not actually encourage kidnapping attempts, certainly furnish the information necessary to undertake them. While the value of such publicity is often very necessary in some areas, such as politics and the world of entertainment, this value must be counterbalanced against the security of those involved. *People in the public eye offer very inviting targets to kidnappers.*

NOTES

1. *Terrorism Part 2,* Hearings before the Committee on Internal Security, House of Representatives (Washington, D.C.: U.S. Government Printing Office, 1974), p. 3120.
2. On this, see H.H.A. Cooper, *Hostage Negotiations: Options and Alternatives,* CTT (Gaithersburg, Md.: International Association of Chiefs of Police, 1978).
3. A notable example occurred in Eire in October, 1975. A Dutch businessman, Dr. Tiede Herrema, was kidnapped by two IRA terrorists. The victim and his captors were discovered by the Irish police in a house just outside Dublin, after which the event became a barricaded hostage situation.
4. Dr. Claude Fly, kidnapped and held for seven months by the Tupamaros in 1970/71, had been warned of the dangers. (Dan Mitrione was taken on the previous Friday.) He recites: "...[they] all pulled guns and they grabbed me and shoved me down the hall and out into the alley. In the struggle they broke my glasses. They blindfolded me, tied my hands and feet, pulled an old gunnysack over my head, threw me in the back of a pickup and drove off." *Terrorism Part 3,* Hearings before the Committee on Internal Security, House of Representatives (Washington, D.C.: U.S. Government Printing Office, 1974), p. 3964.

5. The importance of this is in the negotiating response, for it is valueless offering, in such cases, something *instead* of the victim. Appeals to the abductor have to be launched from a different standpoint.

6. The U.S.I.A., whose officers often serve in very exposed positions, has an excellent program that has substantially improved staff safety in this respect.

7. There is, logically, only an attempted kidnapping which can be frustrated by a number of circumstances, including outside intervention, the escape, or death of the intended victim.

8. Randolph Hearst is reported to have said: "I think the one thing we have in common is that the SLA and I don't want to see my daughter killed."

9. In some instances, the circumstances of the kidnapping are such that considerable risk must be taken in order to convince, as in the case of the Schleyer kidnapping. See *Der Spiegel,* September, 1977.

10. While there is little reason for belief in the general trustworthiness of kidnappers, and there have been cases of ransoms being paid and the victim perishing in the meantime, most kidnappers do keep their bargains. Those who are in this as a business as well as political terrorists cannot afford to acquire a reputation for cheating in this way.

11. For example, of the McKay kidnapping, the first in modern British history, it was said: "The most popular theory argued that Mrs. McKay had staged her own exit from St. Mary House and made her own way back to Australia." Peter Deeley and Christopher Walker, *Murder in the 4th Estate* (New York: McGraw Hill, 1971), p. 57. It took a long while, and an ear, to convince anyone that Eugene Paul Getty II had been kidnapped.

12. Sending a finger or an ear of a kidnap victim is usually intended to be admonitory rather than evidentiary. The receipt of a non-vital part of the body is not intended to set the mind at rest but rather the contrary.

13. For an international overview, see "Comparative Law Aspects of Wiretapping and Electronic Surveillance" in *Commission Studies,* National Wiretapping Commission (Washington, D.C.: U.S. Government Printing Office, 1976), pp. 60-140.

14. There is good and bad in this from the point of view of the

prospects of survival of the victim. If you are conducting a business, even a nefarious one such as kidnapping, you must establish a reputation for being able "to deliver"— too many corpses and no one will deal. On the other hand, victims cannot be kept and "stored" for long periods until the market improves. With the "business" kidnapper, the quicker the deal is made, the better the prospects of survival for the victim.

15. See the observations following the Moro kidnapping in Rome in March, 1978, *Newsweek,* March 27, 1978, p. 66. For an excellent account of a nonpolitical kidnapping, see Curtis Bill Pepper, "Kidnapped," *New York Times Magazine,* November 20, 1977, being a day-by-day relation of the kidnapping of Paolo Lazzaroni.

16. An experienced Italian police officer has said, "Drug smugglers, cigarette smugglers and professional bank robbers often prefer to leave their activities, where risks are much more and the profits limited, and dedicate themselves to cases of abduction where prospects were brighter and more interesting." Antonio Fariello, "The Phenomenon of Hostage Taking: The Italian Experience," *Hostage Taking: Problems of Prevention and Control,* ed. Ronald Crelinsten (Montreal: International Centre for Comparative Criminology, 1976), p. 359.

17. Thus, Larry Flynt, publisher of *Hustler* magazine, shot in Georgia in March, 1978, was "between" bodyguards, having dismissed those formerly in his employ and not yet having engaged new ones.

18. As was tragically the case of the bodyguards of Herr Hanns-Martin Schleyer, kidnapped in Cologne on September 5, 1977, and the bodyguards of Aldo Moro on March 16, 1978.

19. He can, however, be trained to see them, as witness the case of Sir Geoffrey Jackson, kidnap victim of the Tupamaros, whose keen, informed eye led him to detect all the signs of the attempt to be made upon his person.

20. Ambushes are often quite bizarre. A driver, trained in the appropriate techniques might not hesitate to ram an obstructing truck, but how about a baby carriage—as in the case of Herr Schleyer?

21. The technical publications may be consulted for a vast array of excellent equipment now on the market. No spe-

cial recommendation is made here but a caveat is offered that it *must* be of proven reliability, of relatively simple operation, and emergency back-up must be available.

22. It is rarely realized the extent to which the victim is, despite his captivity, master of his own fate. The victim will usually be a person who has been successful in life, and of a higher station and level of intelligence than his captors. If he makes good use of these advantages he may be able to improve his own situation beyond that possible from outside. He may even have to "take charge" of the kidnapper's end of the negotiations for his release. If he can assert himself sufficiently he can be a powerful force in counteracting the adverse effects of panic or despair in his captors. The Lazzaroni kidnapping illustrates this point well; see note 15 above.

23. Sir Geoffrey Jackson, *Surviving the Long Night* (New York: Vanguard Press, 1973), p. 28.

24. In a number of cases in Argentina the victims, mostly high-ranking members of the armed forces, were killed in the attempted kidnappings. The seizures seem, in themselves, to have had the purpose of a symbolic demonstration of power rather than the establishment of a bargaining position. In 1974, Herr von Drenkmann, Chief Justice of West Berlin, was assassinated in what appeared to be an aborted kidnap attempt by West German terrorists.

25. It must not be expected that this will produce any assistance in the way of a rescue attempt, especially in a foreign country, but it is useful in evidencing the event and will provide a useful starting point for any subsequent investigation.

26. A notable case is that of Michael Gordon Jones, U.S. Foreign Service officer who managed to escape from a fast-moving truck although bound and blindfolded, after being kidnapped with great violence on July 31, 1970, by the Tupamaros.

27. Sir Geoffrey was released, ostensibly, because the Tupamaro prisoners, against whose release by the Uruguayan authorities he was held, "escaped" from their place of detention a few days before his release. Accordingly, no further purpose remained in holding him captive, and to have done so might have harmed the Tupamaro cause.

28. The use of force to effect a rescue must be based upon a

proper professional evaluation of the case in hand, not on some preconceived philosophy of how to handle these matters. Compare the damage done by the ill-considered remarks of then Attorney General William Saxbe during the early phase of the Patricia Hearst kidnapping to the effect that the FBI should—if it cornered the SLA—go in and get the victim out.

29. See *Newsweek,* November 14, 1977, p. 82.
30. Kidnappers sometimes make arrangements for the captivity of their victims predicated upon a quick and satisfactory response by those to whom the news of the kidnapping is directed. Delay can be fatal where the kidnappers have allotted comparatively little time for response. See, for example, the case of Barbara Jane Mackle, the Miami student kidnapped in Atlanta in December, 1968, and buried underground. Excellent work by the FBI and prompt family cooperation saved the victim from an agonizing death in the cunningly conceived hideout. Mrs. Gertrude Farber, kidnapped in May, 1977, from her home in Monticello, New York, was not so fortunate. She, too, was buried alive, but suffocated.
31. This should be particularly borne in mind by those who make a business out of the negotiation of ransoms. Laws and practices vary from country to country and consultation with *reliable,* local experts is essential.
32. Such a law was enacted in Argentina, but proved unenforceable. Many systems have laws which attack the matter obliquely and make it, in effect, illegal to enter into dealings of any sort with kidnappers. Prosecutors have tried to use such laws in Italy, particularly Milan, from time to time, but without success.
33. In the case of the kidnapping in Argentina of Oberdan Sallustro, the Fiat executive, "...the Argentina Government warned Fiat executives that they would be prosecuted for 'illicit associations' unless they immediately broke off the ransom contracts with the kidnappers." *Political Kidnappings, 1968-1972* (Washington, D.C.: U.S. Government Printing Office, 1973), p. 24.
34. It should be made clear that the choice for those to whom demands are addressed is often an excruciating one. They are invariably enjoined, from the outset, not to communicate with the authorities on pain of something terrible hap-

pening to the victim on that account. It takes more faith than most have normally in the police—or special training in the need for and advantages of immediate communication—to overcome the effects of that fearful injunction.

35. Caransa is said to have bargained his captors down from 16 million to 4 million dollars.

36. Suffering families, understandably, grasp at straws. A first priority is to find the victim and the services of mediums are often engaged for this purpose. A Dutch medium, for example, was used in the Hearst case, with no noticeable success from a law enforcement point of view.

Hostage Taking

"Hostages! Oh, yes, the Germans knew them well, for having made use of them throughout Europe under the Third Reich."

Serge Groussard[1]

Hostage taking is very similar to kidnapping in many ways, and, indeed, the terms are often used casually as interchangeable even in professional literature. This somewhat promiscuous use of the two terms to cover quite different events is the cause of much confusion and should be avoided. Hostage taking is really quite different from kidnapping in a number of distinctive ways, and different responses are required to each phenomenon. *Hostage taking involves the act of securing total control over the person of another human being for the purpose of ensuring compliance with a pledge made by those interested or obligated in securing the victim's redemption.* In this sense, it is clearly identical with the physical act of kidnapping. There are, however, a number of notable differences that should be observed. In the first place, kidnapping is always a clandestine activity; the effectiveness of the crime depends upon the victim being secreted and held for the purposes of redemption *out of the knowledge and control of those who are trying to effect his release.* Hostage taking is an, *overt act* which has inherently, within it the idea that the acquisition of power over the hostage constitutes, in some measure, a shield for those who have gained this power over the individual concerned. *The value of the hostage's life and physical integrity is interposed as a shield between the hostage-taker and those who would seek to rescue the hostage.* There is, therefore, in every hostage taking, a dual value assigned to the hostage. The primary value of the hostage is as an element of exchange for whatever it is the hostage-taker seeks to strike a bargain about, while the secondary value is to a certain extent even more important, for it is as a shield to safeguard the hostage-taker until the the successful conclusion of his enterprise.

Hostage taking is usually an overt act involving a direct confrontation-type situation with the authorities. It frequently has a deliberate element of drama intended to shock, terrify, or publicize some cause. Unlike kidnapping, it often takes place without any great planning or preparation and is frequently indiscriminate in nature.Kidnapping ususally involves a single individual at any one time as the victim; only in rare cases, such as the Chowchilla kidnapping,[2] are arrangements made for handling and secreting a number of victims. Hostage taking can, and frequently does, involve a large number of victims being reduced into the power of a single captor at any one time. The hostage-taker usually has no immediate intention of taking his victims elsewhere. Multiple hostage takings can be said to be concerned predominately with quantity rather than quality for tactcial reasons; the hostage-taker simply has more with which to bargain. While the situations under which nonpolitical hostage taking is likely to occur are reasonably predictable, for example, frustrated bank robberies, the actual occurrence itself is a much more random event than kidnapping and, consequently, more difficult to prognosticate. The prospects of unintended victimization are greater.

Because of the random nature of hostage taking, it is much more difficult to avoid by preparatory measures than kidnapping. *Anyone can be taken hostage under the most unexpected of circumstances.* Yet much of the advice that would ordinarily be given to those who are potential kidnap victims is applicable to those who are being taken hostage. The drama and immediacy of the situation, however, very often intensify the dangers that the hostage must face. By comparison with kidnapping, hostage taking is usually a short-term event and the pressures and tensions are, correspondingly, concentrated. Additionally, if the victim is taken hostage with a group of other persons, it is possible that he, as an individual, may be selected for ill treatment or even death by the hostage-taker in order to bring pressure upon the authorities. Such selections are not made on a random basis. The best advice, perhaps, that can be given to persons, particularly those in an official position, who have been taken hostage is to *avoid by their actions drawing conspicuous attention to themselves.* The hostage must do everything he can to ensure his survival while those who are working for him from the outside are managing the situation. he must avoid anything likely to precipitate a crisis or make his situation worse.

Because of the nature of the crime, the handling of a hostage-taking incident will be primarily the responsibility of the public law enforcement agencies having jurisdiction in the area where the incident occurs. There will be comparatively little room for intervention by those having the protection of a private individual as their responsibility once that individual has been taken hostage. So far as rescue is concerned, those responsible, in a private capacity, for security of an individual will have a less immediate role in the event of his being taken hostage. Having failed to prevent its occurrence, they can do little to terminate the event on their own account. There will usually be no question of a private negotiation for the release of the hostage. All negotiations will be conducted by the public law enforcement authorities in accordance with the public policy of the place or country where the hostage is taken. If, however, the hostage is seized abroad or the hostage has been taken in the course of a skyjacking, there may well be need for the intervention of a private crisis team, concerned with that individual's security, with a capacity to coordinate its efforts with those of public law enforcement. It could be that an individual taken hostage overseas might be in an extremely difficult position unless the responsible agencies in this country can be persuaded to bring indirect pressure upon the governments concerned, so as to ensure the safety of the individual in question. This is especially the case where a particular hostage, among a group of others in the same predicament, is significantly more valuable or prominent.

An individual already heavily protected against the possiblity of assassination or kidnapping is, naturally, less likely to be taken hostage than one who does not enjoy the benefit of such protective measures. Nevertheless, because of the random nature of the crime, individuals who would ordinarily be well protected against certain eventualities may fall prey to others. Hostage taking is a comparatively rare event in the true terroristic sense, but when it occurs it is of such a character that direct preparation against such a possibility is unlikely to be successful. Preventive measures must, therefore, be focused upon the individual rather than the event, and create in the individual the ability to survive such an experience.

Individuals who are exposed to considerable risk of hostage taking, or of a kidnapping that might turn into a hostage taking as a result of an effective police response, are greatly in need of what might be termed "survival training." Even those moderately exposed, such as bank clerks, could benefit substantially from such instruction. They need to know what it is necessary to do in order to survive the experience effectively. This, very often, means acting against one's natural inclinations, as well as understanding certain phenomena that will almost certainly occur in a majority of cases. What has become known as the "Stockholm Syndrome," or identification with the aggressor, is now reasonably well-known and documented in the literature, although a great deal of research is required to be done into its dynamics.[3] Briefly, what seems to develop under certain circumstances is a feeling of empathy for the captor and his cause that is incongruent with the situation of the victim. In some instances, the victim experiences a sense of abandonment by the authorities and others concerned with his protection and well-being, and begins to see and interpret the event through the eyes of his captors. In extreme cases, the victim can become an obstacle to the successful resolution of the situation. The phenomenon cuts across cultural, sexual, and other boundaries, and even persons in extremely responsible positions are found behaving in this incongruous fashion once they have been reduced into this intense form of captivity.[4]

From the point of view of those engaged in trying to rescue the hostage, it is a good rule never to rely, in any operational sense, upon receiving the cooperation of the hostage, particularly if the hostage situation is a protracted one. The longer the situation continues, the more likely this relationship is to develop and the stronger will be the need for corrective psychological treatment after the situation has been satisfactorily resolved.[5]

In any hostage-taking situation a fundamental principle of survival is to avoid drawing attention to one's self in any way. The obnoxious victim, the "loud mouth," the aggressive personality, or one who stands out as an authority figure, are the ones most likely to be victimized by the hostage-taker in the event of a violent resolution of the matter developing for any reason. Generally, the authorities should avoid giving the impression, in a multiple hostage situation, that one hostage is more valuable or more important to them than any other. This is especially important during any negotiations. The full brunt of the hostage-taker's attentions are likely to fall upon any hostage who is assumed to be more valuable or more important than the rest.[6] Care must be exercised by the authorities to avoid increasing, in any way, the danger in which the hostage already stands by reason of his situation.

The modern phenomenon of skyjacking, the seizure of command of an aircraft in flight, is really no more than a mobile hostage taking. The hostage-taker always faces the problem that, by his act, he becomes himself a prisoner of the situation. He is, effectively, as much a hostage as the victim over whom he has taken immediate control. His action may be defiant and dramatic, such as that of the Palestinian terrorists who took the Israeli athletes hostage at Munich, but his containment makes him a prisoner along with the hostage. He relies upon effecting his escape through a bargain that he can strike with the authorities that will not only give him satisfaction of his primary demands, but will also ensure his escape from the scene to enjoy his triumph. Unless he can do this, the action must be accounted a failure from his perspective. This is a comparatively rare outcome of a hostage-taking situation, and hostage taking has rarely been successful except in a few spectacular cases where organized terrorists have been able to bring to bear sufficient pressure upon the authorities with whom they are dealing to force them to capitulate. Only the strength of public sentiment, and the value placed upon human life in these situations, stand between the hostage-taker and utter failure.

The skyjacking represents a very useful way out of an awkward situation for the hostage-taker, because if he could seize an aircraft in flight and bring it down in friendly or neutral territory, he could then bargain at arm's-length with the authorities for the satisfaction of his demands without having to worry overmuch about his eventual escape. In a theoretical sense, it can be seen that a skyjacking stands midway between a true hostage taking and a kidnapping with regard to the degree of protection afforded the perpetrators. While he is in the air or on friendly soil, the skyjacker clearly has the upper hand, just as the kidnapper does while his hideout or base of operations remain undetected. Some skyjackings have, patently, an original political purpose and are carried out professionally by persons who are often extremely desperate and willing to sacrifice themselves. The skill and dedication of such persons must never be underestimated. The skyjacking of the Japanese Air Lines DC-8 that ended in Algeria in September 1977, which was rapidly followed by the skyjacking of the Lufthansa 737 that ended at Mogadishu, are notable examples of political skyjacking.[7] So, too, were the skyjackings executed by the PFLP that ended in the destruction of a number of commerical aircraft of different nations at Dawson's Field, Jordan, in September 1970.[8] The majority of skyjackings are, however, the work of mentally disturbed individuals, while some are conducted notionally for purely criminal purposes.[9] Skyjacking, like terrorism generally, is a cyclical phenomenon and comparatively few measures can be accounted effective in eradicating it all together. The most useful measure would be the complete denial of safe havens to skyjackers but, for various reasons, this is not possible in the divided political world of today. Skyjacking is, therefore, a phenomenon that is likely to present itself from time to time with varying degrees of intensity and, accordingly, the measures of preparedness that are taken against it should never be relaxed. It must never be assumed that skyjacking has been defeated, or that it will "just go away." From the point of view of individual security, it is as well for persons who are regarded as being in a high-risk category not to travel on commercial airlines at a time when skyjacking is rife and the safety of these is clearly under a considerable threat.

Many top corporation executives and other prominent figures have their own private or business aircraft. It cannot be emphasized too highly that the individual security of these is of the greatest importance. Skyjacking is not necessarily confined to the taking of commerical aircraft. In general, security at general aviation terminals is very lax compared with the protective measures applied to commercial aviation in this country. Overseas, the security may be even less rigorous, and, in consequence, an individual who is accustomed to using his own aircraft may well be unwittingly exposed to a substantial hidden danger requiring considerable attention from those concerned with his protection. This is an aspect that is frequently overlooked. There is a regrettable tendency to regard airports, particularly in the United States, as being relatively heavily protected places. In fact, they are not; and the vigilance of those entrusted with the personal safety of a particular individual should never be relaxed on this account. Similar considerations apply to the protection of the individual's family and loved ones flying by private or corporate aircraft.

As a general rule, it is extremely easy to take hostages. What is more difficult— as many have found to their cost—is to get anything of value for them once they have been seized. The difficulty is not in the physical handling of the hostage, for although some hostage takings have lasted over a period of many days, the operation is generally designed to be of comparatively short duration. The real problem with converting the asset—the hostage—to something else of value is that the action necessarily takes place in a very much more public setting than does a kidnapping, thus leaving less room for subtle maneuver and meaningful negotiation than would be possible where the bulk of the action is taking place behind the scenes. Virtually every facet of the hostage-taking drama is played out in the public arena. A hostage taking is an extremely exposed, very public activity that fulfills—at a price—the terrorist's need for a highly dramatic, symbolic situation. The price of exposure is danger—from which the terrorist can only extricate himself by breaking the resistance of those who, in turn, hold him hostage. A hostage taking is conducted in the glare of publicity, and there are many random factors that can interfere with a successful rescue operation. The great problem for both sides is to avoid taking positions, publicly, from which retraction might not be possible without much loss of face or other inconveniences. The hostage-taker should never be driven into a corner from which it appears the only escape is death.[10] As in dealing with kidnappings, *the watchword is flexibility.* This can only be achieved where there is a very clear understanding of the basic principles involved in the resolution of these situations.

Perhaps the best advice that can be offered to those concerned with the private security of individuals is to recognize the essential difference in their role once the hostage taking has begun from the role they might be called upon to play in the case of a kidnapping. They should arrange to collaborate in every way possible with the public law enforcement authorities and other agencies engaged in trying to secure the victim's safety and release. This is difficult, but particularly needful, where the hostage taking has occurred overseas. They should realize, however, that once a hostage taking has begun, their role will be essentially a subordinate one on all accounts; and they must avoid any form of direct or indirect interference. In particular, their relations with the media, the family and others interested in the safety of the victim require the closest attention. Organizations, whose members are all potential terrorist victims, must avoid public declarations likely to imperil future victims. The situation is marked by the tenseness and the concentration of a great deal of action in a comparatively short period of time. This tends to give the situation a peculiar intensity and makes for very rapid development. Unless there is a considerable understanding of this and preparations are made to meet it, the response will be characterized by much disorganization that could be counterproductive, both from the efforts made by public law enforcement and the prospects of the victim's survival.

NOTES
1. *The Blood of Israel* (New York: William Morrow, 1975), p. 173.

2. This was a bizarre case occurring in July 1976, in which a schoolbus was highjacked and the driver and twenty-six schoolchildren kidnapped. After being driven about in vans for some hours by their kidnappers, the victims were buried in a vehicle that had been prepared for the purpose. They were, fortunately, able to escape through their own endeavors.

3. A great deal has now been written about this interesting phenomenon although it has not been studied to date with the thoroughness the subject deserves. For a good, brief account, see Frederick J. Hacker, *Crusaders, Criminals, Crazies* (New York: W.N. Norton, 1976), pp. 107-112.

4. Most of the serious scientific study to date on the effects of capitvity have related to loss of liberty of lengthy duration, prisoners of war, political detainees, concentration camp victims. Here the loss of liberty is comparatively short but the pressures are intense and fear of death ever-present. There is a real need for serious study of this subject.

5. Considerable experience has been gained by the Dutch authorities in this regard following the train hijackings by the South Moluccans. See, on this, *The Wall Street Journal,* January 6, 1977, pp. 1-3. See, too, *Medical World News,* June 27, 1977, pp. 21-22.

6. This was very graphically demonstrated during the course of a simulated hostage-taking exercise conducted by the IACP in Miami, Florida, on December 8, 1977. The "terrorists," members of Miami Police Department, related in critical detail why they had, under the realistic conditions of the exercise, selected certain victims for particular treatment.

7. See H.H.A. Cooper, "Hostage Rescue Operations: Denouement in Algeria and Mogadishu," *Chitty's Law Journal,* March, 1978.

8. See *The Sky Pirates* (New York: Scribners, 1972).

9. The standard work on this subject is, and will probably remain for some time, *The Skjacker* by David G. Hubbard (New York: Collier, 1973). The depth and magnitude of Dr. Hubbard's work can only be properly appreciated by one who has seen his aircrew training materials and the rich research data on which these are based.

10. Hostage rescue operations should always be approached from the standpoint of offering the hostage-taker *the acceptable alternative*. Much legislation now recognizes this, mitigating the severity of punishment where the hostage-taker surrenders without harming his victim.

Bombing, Firesetting and Contamination

"He put almost no care into the Marine Midland bombing. To judge from what he told me later, he merely assembled a bomb, timed it to go off at 1 a.m., stuck it in a briefcase and wandered down to the financial district to find a good target. It never occurred to him that people might be working in the building when the bomb whent off and, as it happened, a night shift of mostly female typists and clerks was working on two floors of the building during the explosion. A warning call was placed around midnight, but the watchman who answered the call ignored his message. It was mostly luck that the worst that happened was slight injuries to ten or twelve people. Sam had earlier rationalized the possibility of injuring people, in a theoretical discussion, by comparing his activities to the NLF and the Algerians, who carried out revolutionary terrorism in which not only the powerful but also 'innocent bystanders' were injured or killed. But the effect of the actual injuries on him was profound."

Jane Alpert[1]

Destruction of Property

The destruction of tangible property, and the intangible interests associated with it, is the other side of the terrorists' war upon society. Anything of value is considered to be fair game by the terrorist. The destruction of property and other interests may, incidentally, involve the loss of life of those individuals connected with it in some way. In many cases, however, this is an incidental consequence, neither desired nor deliberately sought by those engaged in destroying the property interests. Property has an important symbolic, as well as a material status for society. Property interests are highly prized in an organized society and reflect the social, political, and economic orientation of that society. They form, therefore, a natural point of attack for those claiming to be in opposition to this orientation. Thus, many left-wing terrorist attacks are designed to destroy not merely the actual property interest which is their primary target, but rather the capitalist system of which these interests comprise a significant element. The protection of property from the various onslaughts that can be made upon it is, thus, an important security consideration that goes beyond the actual protection of the property itself. It is, in effect, the defense of the system and its inherent values that are at stake.

Terrorists, particularly those of left-wing persuasion, not infrequently pose an awkward value dilemma for those with property interests. This dilemma is often quite deliberately created for the propaganda value it has for the terrorist cause. To a certain extent, this dilemma is apparent in all kidnapping and hostage-taking situations, where the ostensible value of some property— namely, that which is demanded—is placed in juxtaposition to the value of the human lives in jeopardy. The principles of those engaged in the delicate process of bargaining are held up for all to see. There is an understandable reluctance to part, under circumstances of criminal coercion, with a substantial portion of one's fortune. When this reluctance is set against a human life in peril, the dilemma is starkly evident. It is common to pose the problem in the form that the victim is not regarded as being worth X million dollars by those who are supposedly concerned with his life and are in a position to surrender that sum.[2] This, like much fallacious reasoning, has a superficial attractiveness. The instant victim, in the power of the kidnapper or hostage-taker, can certainly see matters in that light. The real question is much wider and is not concerned so much with the value of a single human life as with the principles behind the bargain that those with control over the victim are seeking to establish and enforce. The real question is always whether one can afford, as a matter of principle, to give in to blackmail. It is a well-stated precept that extortion knows no limits. Once one gives in to a blackmailer, it is said, one can expect only to be bled white. This is why the crime of extortion in all its different forms is so severely dealt with by most systems of positive law; it is a slow death by inches. Nevertheless, there are deep humanitarian considerations involved, and the feelings of the instant victim can never be altogether left out of account. If they were, he might be tempted to strike his own deal with his captors. The value dilemma must be squarely faced, and a compromise with conscience will almost invariably be required.

The dilemma, for those concerned with its resolution, is intensified where property is the primary object of attack. The question then posed is when should the value of property be regarded as so great that human lives are consciously placed in jeopardy for its protection? This is a question that has no convenient philosophical answer. It is a matter of practical economics and social policy that can only be sensibly answered by each value system that is under attack. In a global context, there is much room for a conflict of philosophies within which the individual victim is helplessly caught. The question is crucially highlighted where both lives and property are simultaneously placed in jeopardy, such as in the case of a skyjacking. It must be frankly recognized that the saving of lives may result in the destruction of property, while, conversely, the saving of property may entail a sacrifice of human life.

In those cases where the destruction of property is the primary objective, the terrorist policy in this regard will usually be dictated by fairly self-serving political considerations. The propaganda value of destroying the property of the hated opponent—especially if he can be characterized as a capitalist, imperialist, or exploiter of the "people"—may be sufficient for the purposes of the campaign, whereas the destruction of human life would be counterproductive, propaganda-wise, for those engaged in it. Such considerations have their counterpart in conventional warfare. For this reason, warning is frequently given before property is subject of destructive attack, and the object of this is to ensure that the human beings concerned with it can take refuge or be evacuated. Responsibility for subsequent deaths or injuries can be cast, for propaganda purposes, on those ignoring the warning. Generally, the threat of such attacks alone is usually extremely disruptive so that the evacuation or removal of personnel from a threatened area will take place without the necessity of the actual destruction taking place. There is, thus, a material as well as a propaganda value in such activity. What is affected in these cases is the productive capacity of the asset, and this is sometimes sufficient for the terrorist's purposes. The intangible is destroyed through the threat to the tangible.

The destruction of tangible and intangible property, by terrorists and others, can take many forms and involves the use of many different criminal and terrorist techniques. *Sabotage* is a common technique engaged in both as a result of industrial strife and terroristic activity. It has been greatly developed in modern, irregular warfare. *It involves the deliberate destruction of property of some sort with a view to halting a process that produces or sustains something of value.* It may involve the destruction of machinery, or parts thereof, designed to bring a process to a halt through malfunctioning, or it may involve some deviation from the regular course of the process itself causing a faulty induction fo the energy utilized. The actual details of any form of sabotage, as well as its motivation, will, naturally, depend upon the character of the process itself and the type of property involved. Broadly speaking, it always involves a tampering with something so that it cannot be used in the way that it is intended to be used.

Sabotage may be employed for a variety of reasons. It may be undertaken as a result of a grudge and a desire to interfere with or bring the operations of some organization to an end. It may, on the other hand, have much wider implications and be designed, primarily, to destroy the property and, secondarily, the influence of the organization and its economic capacity. If property cannot be used for the purpose for which it is intended, much of its economic worth is lost. *Sabotage, of itself, is merely a name for the technique.* The actual, violent means used to effect this purpose may be produced by a human being using a knowledge of the process so as to turn the force of the process upon itself, in a destructive way, or may involve actual physical force applied by a human agent alone, or through some type of weapon, tool or machinery. Sometimes fire or explosives will be used to carry out the act of sabotage. Sometimes natural elements, such as water, will be diverted in an unnatural way to spoil or destroy property. Sabotage of transportation can be carried out either by affecting the vehicle itself in some way or by affecting the track or ground over which it runs.[3] Sabotage provides fertile opportunity for the exercise of human ingenuity. The possibilities are almost as diverse as the property and processes that are the subject of attack. Security is rendered exceedingly difficult by reason of the width of these possibilities.

Much property is peculiarly susceptible to damage by fire. Fire is often easily produced by reason of the combustible nature of the property itself, as well as its relatively unprotected state. It is also a highly fearful instrument of attack and produces not only vast destruction in many cases, but also a great deal of terror and anxiety in the community affected. *The malicious destruction of property by fire is called arson*, and this is generally a criminal rather than a terroristic enterprise. Whole communities are sometimes devastated by it, as witness the present state of the South Bronx. Nevertheless, terrorists do, not infrequently, make use of fire as a weapon, and it is peculiarly effective under some circumstances. Fire bombing has been used quite commonly in Northern Ireland.[4] The greatest problem with the use of fire as a terrorist weapon is its indiscriminate quality and the fact that it cannot be effectively controlled and channeled for the destruction of only a limited amount of property. This can be particularly damaging to the terrorist cause, from a propaganda point of view, as the victims are often the constituency to which the terrorist hopes to appeal. Fire, as a terroristic tactical technique, is, perhaps, more useful in a rural than an urban setting. Fire can lay waste to large areas of land, destroying food sources, and is extremely effective where the destruction of other property, such as timber, is intended.[5] Fire set by terrorists is very difficult to bring under control, and the expense of combating it and rehabilitating the area affected is often extremely high in relation to the resources employed to produce the damage. Fire bombing also requires comparatively little skill and experience.

The most usual agent employed by the terrorist for the purposes of causing property destruction and intimidation is generally the explosive device. The use of explosives is capable of producing a massive, terrifying effect upon those likely to be subjected to the destructive forces unleashed. Explosives are also indicated for the destruction of property that by reason of its inherent strength and construction will not yield to other forces. Explosives are very varied in type, quality, potentiality, and use.[6] Their technical qualities and successful employment require considerable study and expert advice. Despite the availability of books, such as those by Kurt Saxon,[7] bomb making and bomb setting are not for amateurs. They are certainly among the most potent weapons employed by terrorist groups. The destructive potential of even a small bomb can be quite considerable.

Every threat to employ explosives must be taken seriously, particularly if those threatening to use them have a past performance indicating the effective use of explosive devices. *The use of explosives always poses a potential threat to human life.* When danger of this sort threatens, it threatens all alike. Bombs are very undiscriminating in their effects, particularly those that have been set with a delayed action timing device. Very often a warning will be given of their use where the objective is principally the destruction of property or the disruption of some activity or process. However, if such a warning is not heeded, or if it is given too late, it is very often the case that the property damage will be accompanied by a loss of human life.[8] The bombsetter can have no control over such a consequence.

From the terrorist's perspective, the destructive potential of the explosive device and its lethal qualities for human beings are really incidental. The primary objective of the terrorist is the creation of massive fear through its employment so that the coercive intentions of the person or organization engineering the situation can be brought into play. Destruction of property on a large scale may be necessary to weaken the enterprise against which the attack is being made, or it may be necessary simply to demonstrate the power of those using the explosives. A well-timed explosion is a convincing demonstration of that power. *Whatever the purpose, every bomb carries its own message.* The task of the terrorist is to make sure that message is received and understood.

The use of anything other than the most primitive of explosive devices usually calls for considerable organization and skill among those employing this type of weapon. Certainly, this is the case where terrorists engage in a systematic bombing campaign. There is very often a marked division of labor, with some persons specializing in the design of explosive artifacts, others engaged in their actual fabrication, while still others will be concerned with their transportation and placement in the locations that are earmarked for destruction. Other agents yet will be concerned with the acquisition of explosive materials. Different skills are needed for each operation. All this adds up to a very high degree of organization and a certain vulnerability at different points in the various processes. This fact should be noted by those engaged in designing countermeasures. Many of the individuals engaged in the more technical aspects of this work will have received military training or will have had some sort of civilian employment that can be adapted or converted for these purposes. They will often add a distinctive touch or "trademark" that is important for investigative purposes. The number of persons who can engage in the skilled fabrication of some of the more complicated devices is comparatively small. This fact, fortunately, limits the more serious terroristic enterprises.

Over the years, technology has provided the bomb maker with a variety of new possibilities to employ in the exercise of his craft.[9] In particular, many explosives have become very much more powerful, while at the same time taking up less space and weighing less. New explosive materials that can be more safely handled have now become available to the terrorist bomber. This means that much more powerful explosive devices can be made with less material that they can be transported with less difficulty than formerly. Nevertheless, many explosives in use by terrorists are still fairly primitive, are made from easily obtainable materials, and involve the use of quantity rather than quality to achieve their explosive effect. Such practices and procedures should not, however, be held in contempt. Even a somewhat unsophisticated explosive device is still capable of creating great damage and loss of life. If enough of such devices are used on a frequent basis, their disruptive effect can be enormous. The humble pipe bomb must be considered to have a great deal more than mere nuisance value.

The detection of explosive devices can be conducted by relatively unskilled personnel using correct procedures for the purpose. Alert personnel with a knowledge of what to look for can save lives and much property damage.[10] The disarming of the explosive devices is a matter for the expert. *The amateur should never tamper with, or indeed handle, a recognized explosive device of any kind.* Once an explosive device has been detected, all personnel should be smoothly and rapidly evacuated from the scene. Bombs should only be handled by properly trained and equipped explosive ordnance disposal technicians.

In a certain sense, bombing property has much in common with kidnapping. Both are, essentially, covert or clandestine activities. The bomb, like the kidnap victim, is usually hidden and owes much of its potential lethality to the fact that it is in an unknown location. Those who are subjected to the threat of its being exploded are unaware of its precise location and are powerless to do anything about it on that account. The coercive power of the bomber lies in his knowledge of where the device has been placed and when it is set to explode. Once the explosive device has been detected, however, proper steps can be taken to neutralize its destructive potential and to limit the advantages that those who have placed it would seek to gain. *Finding the explosive device is, therefore, a first priority.* Disarming it is a matter of time and technique.

Not all bombing is clandestine. Some bombs are still thrown in public places, but these generally involve attacks on people rather than property.[11] Nonconfrontation type of bombing is a tactic frequently engaged in by terrorist groups when they will feel relatively weak and are unable to engage their adversary frontally. It is also a tactic to which resort is made when the countermeasures have been so effective that other options are drastically reduced. It is noteworthy that the West German terrorists turned once more to bombing and threatened destruction of aircraft after their campaign of assassination and kidnapping had failed to achieve its goals. Bombing is currently the most serious threat posed in the United States by domestic terdrorist groups. The incidence of bombing is, in some measure, a reflection of the state of terrorism in any particular society at any particular time. It is an excellent indicator of the technical capacity as well as the philosophy of terrorist groups. As a general matter, it may be observed that as the level of the terrorists' frustration rises and they are unable to achieve their objectives by other methods, the level of indiscriminate bombing, where little regard is paid to human life, rises. The history of the various Palestinian terrorist movements may usefully be examined in this regard. In situations where wuch a degree of desperation is reached that the primary objective is mass destruction at all costs, respect for human life diminishes to zero. This generally occurs where the political advantages of terror and chaos are felt to out weigh the negative political consequences of such callousness. As a consequence, bombs are placed without warning, their destructive potential is greatly increased, and their use is coupled with a deliberate campaign designed to expressly intimidate through the calculated destruction of human life as well as property. In such cases, personnel bombs are used or ordinary explosive devices are modified to include an anti-personnel element. Such campaigns are usually mounted by groups having a nihilistic or anarchistic political philosophy, by foreign groups, or against foreigners in some overseas territory.

Sometimes the attack upon an intangible interest by means of a bombing campaign is directed primarily at the human element concerned with operating the interest or the process involved. The objective is intimidation so that the process is brought to a halt or ordinary human relations jeopardized. Typical of this is the use of the mail bomb. Here, a small though powerful explosive device designed primarily to kill or maim a human being, is secreted in a mailed envelope or package so that when it is opened it will kill or injure the human being to whom it is addressed or some subordinate who would be entrusted with opening the communication. A female secretary employed by the British Embassy in Washington, D.C., lost a hand as a result of a mail bomb in 1973. A mail bombing campaign has a marked intimidatory effect and can result in a number of deaths through imperfect security measures or the surprise of the attack itself. It is relatively economical and allows for a destructive potential to be spread over a large area by a relatively small number of persons. Sometimes, specific targets are selected, while at other times mailings are quite indiscriminate. It is extremely dramatic and causes widespread fear even among those unlikely to be the recipients of the bomb itself. Mail bombing campaigns have been mounted by the IRA, as well as Arab terrorists. New, improved types of explosive devices are now in being, and their use must be anticipated in any future campaign.

Other more direct attacks upon personnel include car bombings, where a particular individual is selected for assassination by the use of an explosive device secreted in a vehicle. Car bombings can be very spectacular and especially frightening. The device is often constructed so as to explode when certain action, such as starting the car, is taken. Sometimes such devices are electronically detonated by means of an external source. Car bombings are sometimes undertaken with great sophistication and precision, shaped charges being employed, such as that which took the life of Orlando Letelier, former Chilean Ambassador to the United States, in Washington, D.C. in 1976. In all these cases, the intangible property interest is attacked indirectly through the human beings who are associated with it. The value of the property diminishes because of the peril to which the human element that would utilize it is exposed. Effective countermeasures depend primarily upon alert, well-informed personnel and effective search and screening procedures. It must be recognized that it is possible to tamper with any vehicle left, for however short a time, in an unprotected setting.

In the future, it may be anticipated that weapons of even greater destructive, explosive potential than hitherto employed by terrorists will be utilized. *The use by terrorists of nuclear weapons or the threat of their use is a very real prospect within the next few years.*[12] This eventuality must be realistically taken into account, not only by single enterprises that might be the direct targets, but whole communities that will fall under the threat of the mass destruction capable of being caused. The ability to acquire, produce, and utilize weapons of mass destruction by small, organized terrorist groups must now be accounted as a fact. That they have not yet been used by such groups must not be taken as evidence at they do not presently have this capacity. The employment of weapons of mass destruction has its drawbacks for those concerned with preserving a certain political image or with reducing the number of casualties, but for those driven to a position of desperation or who feel the desirability of entering into a struggle on this scale, the use of such weapons must be accounted a real possibility. Their employment would constitute a desperate gamble and might well be regarded by them as a "one-shot" operation. The use of such weapons would constitute a challenge to power on a massive scale, and success in their employment would be tantamount to bringing government and society, as we understand it, virtually to an end. To certain kinds of minds, there is a great attractiveness in all this that cannot be overlooked. The material and psychological potential is clearly available for a greatly enhanced terrorist activity in this area. The closest cooperation between public and private security is necessary to meet the challenge.

When the overall effectiveness of bombing as a terroristic tactic or technique is examined, it is surprising, at first sight, that so little takes place. It is relatively economical and of great potential. It would appear to be favorable to the terrorist's interests to step up bombing to such an extent that the system would be overwhelmed. In theory, this could be done; but in practice it never seems to take place even in situations of near civil war, such as Northern Ireland. There are a number of reasons for this, some sociological and others psychological. The most effective materials for the fabrication of explosive devices are not as easy to come by as some of the more bizarre literature would seem to suggest. While it is sometimes possible to steal military material, there is always the problem of storage and handling. A high degree of technical knowledge is necessary, and this, fortunately, resides in a comparatively few people. Explosives are dangerous for those who would use them, as many have found to their cost.[13] There is something fearsome about undertaking bombing—and particularly bomb making— on a cold-blooded basis that appeals to a comparatively few minds. Sometimes the requisite knowledge is not matched by the appropriate degree of callousness. In short, there is a shortage of skills, a shortage of materials, and a shortage of the necessary viciousness to undertake the task. There are many other complex psychological, as well as political, factors that tend to have a limiting effect. It is simply too impersonal and indiscriminate for many. Fortunately, bombing, even under the most extreme of political conditions, rarely reaches proportions where it would bring life and business to a standstill or where it would get out of complete control by those engaged in taking countermeasures against it. As shown by conventional warfare, people and places can take a great deal of bombing.

Nevertheless, bombing, whether systematic or sporadic, is probably one of the most serious threats to security that the individual and the community can face. It is, perhaps, easier to undertake a bombing campaign than it is to provide protection against one. It requires very special methods of protection that are the subject of extremely specialized and detailed treatment. The necessary skills are the fruit of long apprenticeship and experience. It cannot be overemphasized that the handling of a bombing threat, whether issued by criminal elements or terrorists, is a job for specialists. Whatever the capacity of an organization to handle other types of security problems, it is unwise to attempt to handle a campaign in which terrorists make use of explosive devices, without recourse to specialist advice and operational capabilities. This is so not only with regard to the handling, dismantling and disposal of explosive devices actually discovered, but with regard to all phases of protective planning and prevention. The determined terrorist can do a great deal of damage, human and material, with explosive devices. Such determination must be met with equal determination and skill in the planning and preparation of security measures. While the actual destruction of property caused by an explosive device can be great and may also involve loss of human life, the mere threat can often be as disruptive as any other tactic or technique in the terrorist armory. Carlos Marighella strongly advocates the systematic use of threats for disruptive purposes.[14] *The great problem with threats is knowing how to distinguish what is serious from what is bluff.* This, again, is a very skilled business. Much modern technology, especially in the area of psycholinguistics, is used to tell the true from the false. As with all terrorist threats, the watchword is: *be prepared.* The important thing is to take the right type of precautions. Due to the tremendous potentiality for the use of explosive devices by terrorists and others, being prepared involves a great deal more by way of precautions than those that might be taken usefully against other eventualities.

Only the barest outline of what is involved in planning and preparation to meet a bombing threat is given here. A more exact idea can be obtained from reading specialist literature on the subject.[15] This latter should never, however, be substituted for the proper, professional advice. It is reiterated that solutions of security problems cannot be general, but must be custom-made to each situation and will invariably require detailed specialist advice and execution. Bombing will often take place against a general atmosphere of chaos and confusion. It is an extreme crisis management situation. Important decisions have to be made, often with little time to process or verify available information. A bomb threat is like any other crisis. It requires that calm, useful decisions be taken under pressure by those responsible. The only way this can be successfully done is for those responsible to understand, clearly, the nature of their responsibilities and where they can turn to for help when the need arises. Every organization faced with a terrorist threat should have a top-level *crisis management team* capable of evaluating the threat and its implications, and issuing the necessary directives to meet it. So far as bombings are concerned, it must be capable of responding very quickly. Time will often be of the essence. Decisions have to be made to evacuate personnel, to call into operation various public emergency services, to close down certain processes, and to respond to demands made in consequence of the threat. Well thought out procedures can save much operational confusion. A crisis team created in the middle of a crisis cannot be expected to work as well as one that has anticipated the event and prepared for it.

Noxious Substances

Next to explosives, perhaps the most fearful weapon available to terrorists is that comprised by the wide category of toxic substances of a chemical or bacteriological nature. By comparison with explosives, these substances constitute a somewhat exotic range of materials and their employment by terrorists is, consequently, much less common.[16] The potential for mass destruction of life and property, and the accompanying terror, is, however, no less great. In some cases, given the right conditions, chemical or bacteriological warfare is the better option.[17] Many industrial and business operations are extremely vulnerable to attack by this means. Real protection is costly and difficult to establish. Individuals can readily be assassinated by poisonous substances employed in various ways, and the dramatic focus upon this in recent times through the activities of governments has certainly promoted ideas among terrorist groups that may well find their place in eventual action. Poison can be administered equally well by men or women though it has certain advantages that make its use by women peculiarly attractive. Poisoning, whether by means of organic or inorganic chemical substances, or bacteriological material, is the essence of clandestine activity. The secretive, unknown nature of the activity and the horrible forms of death that can ensue are particularly fear-producing and, accordingly, well adapted to terroristic purposes. Even the threat of the employment of such substances can give rise to widespread panic.

Assassination by poisoning is almost as old as politics itself. History books abound with models that serve as illustration to the modern terrorist. Almost infinite opportunities are available for poisoning either individuals or random samples of the community. The ways in which these substances can be introduced into the human body are limited only by the imagination. It is, again, fortunate that terrorists do not exploit these possibilities as much as they might, and one can only speculate on the reasons for this reticence.[18] The possibilities that exist for the terroristic use of noxious substances against individuals or the community at large are immense, and it is extremely difficult to develop effective protective measures against them in advance. Some of the substances that might be used are, practically, almost impossible to detect, and it is extremely difficult to erect any form of protection against them. Many of the substances, too, are extremely quick-acting and could be used to devastating effect by those who had the skill and malicious intent necessary for their employment.

Curiously enough, chemical and bacteriological warfare has never been very popular even in the conventional sense. This is not due to doubts about the lethal potentiality of the substances involved. The real difficulty lies not so much in the availability of knowledge about these materials and how to manufacture them than in the logistical problems of controlling the deployment and targeting of these substances for warlike purposes. Terrorists experience very much the same difficulties. It is, put simply, extremely hard to project or direct some of these substances in a concentrated fashion so that they might do the harm of which they are theoretically capable. There is also a great and understandable fear among people, generally, regarding the use of such substances, and these fears tend to inhibit their practical employment. There is great fear of the unknown, and this can only be overcome by an experimentation of which few are capable. Before noxious substances can be usefully employed by terrorists, they must be acquired, prepared or put in a form in which they can be used, transported to the scene, and then deployed in a form which can be effective against the target. This requires a great deal of technical skill as well as favorable circumstances for the employment of this very sophisticated type of weaponry. Much preparatory work and a certain amount of laboratory testing is needed. The difficulties involved in obtaining such a conjunction of circumstances very often make the use of other methods more attractive. Terrorists generally seek the easy way out.

So far as the security of individuals is concerned, a number of general observations can be offered. They will most often be the subject of poisoning by relatively conventional—and easily obtained—substances of an organic or nonorganic character. Some, like cyanide compounds, are very quick-acting, so that their effects may be immediately apparent. They can, however, be mistaken for something else. KGB agents have used cyanide substances under circumstances where the victim was assumed to have died from natural causes.[19] Some substances are capable of being transmitted or conveyed by the atmosphere, for example, as dust particles, while others must be introduced into the food or water, or placed upon the skin or clothing of the individual to be poisoned.[20] Sometimes more than one substance is administered so as to disguise the nature of the poisoning. Other noxious substances can be painted onto articles of common use that are likely to be touched by the intended victim. Not all noxious substances are poisonous in the strict sense. Powdered glass in food can devastate the intestinal tract and cause severe hemorrhaging. Air injected into the bloodstream can cause a fatal embolism. Poisonous snakes or insects can be sent to the victim so that he inadvertently handles them. Only in those cases where the poisonous substance can be directly administered to the victim either by way of food or drink, or injected into him, or placed directly upon his clothing, can it be certain that other persons will not be affected. This, of course, is only of importance where it is intended to assassinate a single individual by these means. Where those who are using these substances are quite indifferent to the amount of death or suffering they might cause, provided the intended victim is among those eliminated, any of the substances that need a more extended distribution can be effectively used. Indiscriminate distribution is often part of a generalized terror campaign.

Protection against such a diversity of possibilities is extremely difficult as in the worst of cases, the precautions that have to be taken, in themselves, generate in the target subject and others what amounts to a high degree of paranoia. The use of food tasters and all sorts of screening processs can reduce the quality of life almost to zero for the individual who has to be protected in this way. Fear and uncertainty prey on the mind of the threatened subject in a most debilitating way. Even with the most stringent precautions, it is always possible that a noxious substance can be introduced by someone who is sufficiently determined to kill the victim in this way. The assassin will study well the habits of his victim and will adapt his technique and the substance he employs accordingly. Certain common sense procedures should always be taken, particularly where food preparation and serving are concerned, while the receipt of unexpected gifts, particularly comestibles, should be treated in very much the same way as the receipt of unsolicited materials of any sort that might contain an explosive device. Revenge killings, particularly in prisons, have often made use of the victim's curiosity or gluttony by sending him poisoned foodstuffs. Once more, it is evident that the true power of the terrorist who chooses to employ this weapon lies in its clandestine nature. Terrorism is aided by the unexpected. The unknown nature and appearance of the substance and the fact that it might be contained or employed anywhere is the potent threat upon which the generation of fear rests. The mere fact that handling the most ordinary of substances might be deadly for the person so engaged is an extremely potent, fear-producing weapons. The great value of this for terrorists lies in the fact that lethal substances really can be easily introduced and concealed and defy detection by ordinary screening methods. Their use is no bizarre or unlikely eventuality. Persons whose daily regimen is such that they have no control over the food and drink they partake are particularly susceptible to having noxious substances introduced at any time in such a way that protective measures, even of a common sense character, are virtually useless. Travelers and others who must accept hospitality are very vulnerable as also are those serving overseas under circumstances where strict and constant supervision of all daily needs of life is impossible. In the case of a quick-acting, virtually tasteless substance, even the victim's own perceptions will fail to serve as a defense. The appropriate antidote is not usually available even if a correct diagnosis has been speedily made.

The possibility of large-scale destruction by the use of these deadly means on a random basis is ever present, and must be a source of ever-growing concern to public law enforcement officials and those charged with the provision of protective services. If the individual is extremely vulnerable due to the lack of adequate screening defenses and the need for living a relatively normal life free from the sort of protection that would have a socially inhibiting, as well as an adverse psychological, effect it is obvious that the community is even more so. Food supplies and water supplies are particularly vulnerable to attack by noxious substances of many types, and the already contaminated atmosphere that we have become used to breathing each day can easily be subtly contaminated further in a truly lethal fashion by one having the knowledge and capacity to do so. Some of the more exotic materials that can be used for these purposes literally defy common analysis, and certainly there is no known protection or antidote that could secure a community against them. Detection of such substances by other than very complicated equipment, operating very selectively, is virtually impossible.

While the general unavailability of these substances and the lack of requisite knowledge in their preparation and use undoubtedly precludes many terrorists from employing them, there must realistically be taken into account a corresponding risk to the community generally from the lone psychopath or simply one having a grudge for these substances are readily concealable, utilizable in a way that would defy most forms of detection, and require little by way of organization to be able to make the desired impact. There are attractive weapons available to the loner, and it is worth his while to take the time and care necessary to inform himself about them.[21] The knowledge and the means are sometimes more formally acquired. There are many chemicals and biological agents that can be obtained for the purposes of indiscriminate dissemination so as to produce harmful effects, and there are many persons who have been officially trained in their use for other purposes and upon whose stability, loyalty and good sense we cannot rely absolutely. There are many opportunities for frightening, individual action in this area. The possibility that such individuals might be lurking among us is dramatically illustrated by the so-called Legionnaires Disease which drastically hit a convention hotel in Philadelphia during the Bicentennial celebration, and has subsequently reemerged in other places since 1976.[22]

The use of radioactive materials, such as plutonium dust, cannot be discounted as a terrorist possibility.[23] Indeed, one of the arguments advanced against the fast-breeder reactor is that its use would facilitate the illicit acquisition of plutonium by terrorists.[24] If the terrorists should move into a phase of indiscriminate mass destruction, then the use of a relatively slow-acting agent of this sort, on a large scale, could be quite devastating. A substantial population could be decimated through the effects of radioactivity before it was realized what had caused it. It is not necessary to consider here what benefit might be derived from the employment of such substances, but the desperation of those who have tried other means of social disruption, and failed, may well lead them to employ agents of a more exotic and lethal character. The damage that could be produced by the appropriate dissemination of radioactive dust of this kind would probably be almost as great as what might be produced by the type of explosive nuclear device that terrorists presently have the capability of making and deploying. Reservoirs, supply tanks, and conduit pipes are often very vulnerable. The possibility of contaminating the public water supply with a lethal substance has been canvassed on a number of occasions, but, generally speaking, most of the chemical agents suggested have too short an effective life to do the harm anticipated. Although LSD is highly toxic in microscopic quantities, its instability precludes its use for these purposes. Nevertheless, the possibility of such an eventuality must be taken seriously into account, and food and water supplies must be regarded as particularly vulnerable to attack by alkaloids that can be relatively easily obtained and even more easily introduced into substances that will be consumed by human beings and animals.[25] Some of these substances are of innocent appearance and can be transported and handled without giving rise to suspicion. While many chemicals are indeed very unstable, even they might be worth experimenting with on the part of terrorists in order to see what type of effect they might have. The terrorist has a large laboratory at his disposal and one of the customary restraints upon experimentation with human beings. The type of covert experiments with noxious substances that have been undertaken by United States government agencies are suggestive of these possibilities, and terroristic imitation of them is only to be realistically expected.[26]

The use of chemical agents and other forms of destructive bacteria against plant life and agricultural crops must also be considered a possibility in any terrorist campaign. Defoliation agents have been used, with mixed success, in conventional warfare; and in the event of a terroristic enterprise of any magnitude, it must be expected that there will be strikes, not only against energy sources, but also against food supplies. Domestic animals can be poisoned or infected with disease. Their food and water supplies are usually extremely exposed. Crops can be contaminated before reaching the industrial processes necessary to convert them into food, and this could have a devastating effect upon the populace. The resultant shortages and uncertainty could lead to civil disorders capable of being exploited by terrorists. Even the threat of introducing harmful substances into raw or prepared food products might be sufficient to cause its withdrawal and very considerable economic losses to those

106

who are involved in the process.[27] The detection of such substances is very difficult and general precautionary measures against their employment extremely expensive.

The possibility of terrorists using highly toxic substances, such as anthrax spores or cryptococcosis, in high density buildings and working areas should also be considered.[28] These substances, like plutonium dust, or even nerve gases, could be relatively easily introduced into ventilation systems and air ducts in such a way that their effects would spread very rapidly and uniformly throughout the entire building. Various chemical combinations can be used to the same end. This would not only bring all activities within the building to a halt, but would cause considerable casualties and much panic. Moreover, the resultant publicity might give rise to imitation elsewhere. An example of the potentiality of this on a much lower lethal scale can be seen from the disruption caused to the operations of the Washington, D.C. Metropolitan Police, as a result of an explosion of tear gas canisters in the District Building in January 1978. The building was rendered largely unusable for a considerable number of days and the gas produced much discomfort to those who were exposed to it. Had the gas in question been of a truly lethal character, the resulting chaos would have been enormous, and such a possibility in consequence of terrorist action must always be considered. Wherever large crowds gather, in the open or indoors, such as theatres, race tracks, or athletic stadiums, there exists a vulnerability to attack by these means.

To a certain extent, the possibility of poisonous gas being introduced into a highly sensitive atmosphere can be guarded against by having the appropriate masking equipment available, together with supplies of oxygen and other medical equipment to counter its effects and treat casualties. Many gases, however, cannot be readily detected, and the terrorists' advantages of surprise and initiative would make an attack virtually irresistible. The possibilities of an attack,, making use of a noxious substance of some sort, involving large city buildings must always be accounted a realistic possibility, for the amount of disruption that can be economically produced by using even a single operative is much greater than could be contemplated in such cases by the use of explosive devices.

The debilitating effects of poisoning, particularly that caused by micro-organisms such as botulism or salmonella, on a population already subjected to fearful attacks of another kind of terrorist group must be taken into consideration. Not only is it extremely difficult to guard against such contamination, but the resultant fear of not knowing what is causing the problem can be very great and collectively disorganizing. In 1951, a small village in France, Pont St. Esprit, was affected in this way by an alkaloid that appears to have contaminated flour used for bread making.[29] The consequent chaos that affected that community could easily be duplicated by terroristic action, and it is well for these possibilities to be realistically considered. The amount of laboratory analysis necessary over a long period to determine the cause of the harm to the community is often so extended that important decisions regarding it cannot be taken. Protection cannot be conveniently provided against the unknown. What cannot be made known quickly enough might well be fatal before its nature and origins are discovered.

NOTES

1. *Letters From Attica by Samuel Melville* (New York: William Morrow, 1972), p. 29.

2. The practical consequences of this should never be overlooked. It is a chilling revelation to the victim, unless he has been professionally prepared beforehand, to find that, in pecuniary terms, he is not worth as much as he had supposed. Families have been torn asunder by this practical demonstration of their values.

3. A series of disastrous train derailments in the United States in 1978 recalls the following: "To sabotage railroad lines requires only the simplest equipment, crow bars and sledge hammers. To derail a train all that is necessary is to loosen the tie mounting on eight successive ties. Remove the fishplate and apply leverage with a crow bar so as to move one rail toward the inside. Jam the fishplate in between." Geroge Prosser, *Terrorism, Part 2,* Exhibit No. 13, pp. 63-64. The IRA recommends: "Unbolt railway lines at an embankment or on a gradient or curve. This tilts the train off the lines for a considerable time." *Handbook for Volunteers of the Irish Republican Army,* 1956, Reprinted in C.T.T. (Gaithersburg, Md.: International Association of Chiefs of Police, 1974), p. 29.

4. Much of the major damage in the center of Belfast has been done by firebombs, particularly to department stores which are often gutted. The original act of the

Baader-Meinhof group was the firebombing of department stores in Frankfurt.

5. The Russians have made effective use of a "scorched earth" policy since the time of Peter the Great. It has been effectively copied as a technique of irregular warfare in many countries and is to be found in most guerrilla manuals.

6. For a good overview, see Thomas G. Brodie, *Bombs and Bombings* (Springfield, Ill.: Charles C. Thomas, 1973).

7. For example, *Fireworks and Explosives Like Grandad Used To Make* (Eureka, Cal.: Atlan Formularies, 1975). See, especially, pp. 44-50.

8. In July 1946, the Irgun Zvai Leumi, a right wing Jewish terrorist group headed by Menachem Begin, now Prime Minister of Israel, planted a bomb in the basement of the King David Hotel in Jerusalem. There is some controversy over whether a warning was given at all, but the result of the tremendous explosion was ninety-one persons killed, forty-five injured and a lasting resentment against those responsible. For a very balanced account, see J. Bowyer Bell, *Terror Out of Zion* (New York: St. Martin's Press, 1977), pp. 169-173.

9. See, for example, Robert R. Lenz, *Explosives and Bomb Disposal Guide* (Springfield, Ill.: Charles C. Thomas, 1973). See, also, C.R. Newhouser, *Mail Bombs,* C.T.T. (Gaithersburg, Md.: International Association of Chiefs of Police, 1973).

10. The IRA bombing campaigns have certainly sharpened the senses of those subjected to them. Suitcases and carrier bags left unattended arouse immediate suspicion as do vehicles parked in and around sensitive areas. These are skills that are developed by necessity and tend to become dulled through lack of exercise.

11. For example, on September 15, 1974, a young man dropped a U.S. made hand grenade among customers at Le Drugstore, a combined boutique, newsstand and snack bar on the Boulevard St. Germain, Paris, killing two persons and wounding thirty-four others. The event was curiously reminiscent of the anarchist bombings in Paris at the end of the last century.

12. Several amateurish threats have been made in the past few years. The success with which their handling was blessed

stemmed less from the system constructed to handle them than their basic lack of substance. Soon, we may be faced with a threat that is not based on bluff. That the capability is there is a conclusion drawn by most reliable observers. See R.W. Mengel, "Terrorism and New Technologies of Destruction: An Overview of the Potential Risk," Appendix 2 of *Disorders and Terrorism* (Wash., D.C.: U.S. Gov't Printing Office, 1977).

13. This is due not only to the hazardous conditions under which bombs are made and assembled, but to inexperience and carelessness. It has been pertinently written: "Many bomb makers take incredible risks." John M. MacDonald, *Bombers and Firesetters* (Springfield, Ill.: Charles C. Thomas, 1977), p. 28. The explosion in the Greenwich Village townhouse on March 6, 1970, that killed three members of the Weather Underground is instructive in this regard.

14. In the oft-cited, frequently reprinted and much excerpted *Minimanual of the Urban Guerilla* (Havana, Cuba: Tricontinental, 1970).

15. See, for example, *Bomb Incident Management* (Gaithersburg, Md.: International Association of Chiefs of Police, 1973).

16. See, for an excellent synopsis, R.W. Mengel, "Terrorism and New Technologies of Destruction: An Overview of the Potential Risk," Appendix 2 of *Disorders and Terrorism* (Washington, D.C.: U.S. Government Printing Office, 1977).

17. "Toxic agents offer great potential as effective sabotage weapons. Sabotage committed with them could destroy confidence in the ability of our government to insure the protection of our food, medicines and the like." J.H. Rothschild, *Tomorrow's Weapons* (New York: McGraw Hill, 1964), pp. 132-133.

18. Those who write about these matters generally do so with undisguised enthusiasm. See Kurt Saxon, *The Poor Man's James Bond* (Eureka, Cal.: Atlan Formularies, 1972), pp. 39-48. See, also, John Minnery, *How to Kill* (Boulder, Colo.: Paladin Press, 1973), pp. 41-43.

19. On this, see J. David Truby and John Minnery, *Improvised Modified Firearms,* Vol. II (Boulder, Colo.: Paladin Press, 1975), pp. 30-31. There have been suspicions of organized crime killings in New Jersey using similar means.

20. See, for example, William Joseph Ward, "DMSO: A New Threat in Public Figure Protection?" *Assets Protection,* No. 3, 1976, pp. 11-15.

21. There is, unfortunately, no lack of literature available on the subject. Some of it is frankly tendentious and calculated to act upon the minds of those who might be prone to experiment. It is difficult to estimate the impact of this material, but its availability has been a matter of concern to experts.

22. There has been much speculation on this. See, for example, "Scandal in Philadelphia," *Assassin,* Vol. 1, No. 1, 1977, pp. 6-20.

23. See, for example, David Krieger, "What Happens If...? Terrorists, Revolutionaries and Nuclear Weapons," 430 *The Annals,* March, 1977, pp. 44-57, especially p. 53.

24. "...But it is probably going to prove wise to have slowed the advance of plutonium in terrorists' hands." *The Economist,* May 21, 1977, p. 13.

25. There was at one time a much publicized plan by RAM (Revolutionary Action Movement) to poison the water supply of Philadelphia, but, happily, it did not materialize. Threats have been made by other groups at other cities from time to time.

26. See Lowell Ponte, "Warning! Welcome to the Coming Nightmare Decade of the Terrorists' War on American Cities," *Gallery,* May, 1977, p. 37.

27. The discovery in the Netherlands in January 1978 of Israeli oranges into which liquid mercury had been injected was the cause of considerable and widespread concern. This, though amateurish, was indicative of the inherent possibilities open to more knowledgeable and determined perpetrators. See *New York Times,* February 2, 1978, p. A2.

28. See *Disorders and Terrorism* (Washington, D.C.: U.S. Government Printing office, 1977), p. 447.

29. For this remarkable and thought provoking episode, see John G. Fuller, *The Day of St. Anthony's Fire* (New York: Macmillian, 1968).

Extortion

"Even as a young man, Vito Corleone became known as a 'man of reasonableness.' He never uttered a threat. He always used logic that proved to be irresistible. He always made certain that the other fellow got his share of profit. Nobody lost. He did this, of course, by obvious means. Like many businessmen of genius he learned that free competition was wasteful, monopoly efficient. And so he simply set about achieving that efficient monopoly. There were some oil wholesalers in Brooklyn, men of fiery temper, headstrong, not amenable to reason, who refused to see, to recognize, the vision of Vito Corleone, even after he had explained everything to them with the utmost patience and detail. With these men Vito Corleone threw up his hands in despair and sent Tessio to Brooklyn to set up a headquarters and solve the problem. Warehouses were burned, truckloads of olive-green oil were dumped to form lakes in the cobbled waterfront streets. One rash man, an arrogant Milanese with more faith in the police than a saint has in Christ, actually went to the authorities with a complaint against his fellow Italians, breaking the ten-century-old law of omerta. But before the matter could proceed further, the wholesaler disappeared, never to been seen again, leaving behind, deserted, his devoted wife and three children, who, God be thanked, were fully grown and capable of taking over his business and coming to terms with the Genco Pura Oil Company."

Mario Puzo[1]

It takes money to engage in even the shortest, most inexpensive war. Most terroristic enterprises seek to benefit in some material way from the threat to life and property which they pose. Terrorists, like organized crime, have to bankroll their operations. They cannot always rely on the support of a rich, ideologically compatible philanthropist. While some terrorist operations may be simply symbolic or designed merely to put an end to a state of affairs that the terrorists consider intolerable, other activities will be organized so as to set up a bargaining situation. Whatever terrorist ideology may have to say about the principle of enrichment, soaking the rich to give to the poor always has a popular appeal. The early popularity of the Tupamaros in Uruguay was due to a careful cultivation of this "Robin Hood" image.[2] *At the very heart of these activities lies the crime of extortion.* This is very clearly indicated in the case of kidnappings and hostage takings, but other activity too, such as bombing, may have as its purpose the illicit derivation of wealth or other advantages to be gained from putting an asset at risk.[3] The motivation may be twofold. In the first place, any successful extortion is bound to weaken those whom the terrorists regard as enemies. It constitutes a significant wasting of the enemy's assets. Some ransoms have been enormous in relation to total assets.[4] In the second place, the contributed assets go to fortify the terrorists' own position. Many money ransoms are utilized to build up a war chest and, in general, increase the terrorists' capacity for harm.

Extortion should be seen as part of the wider power play by terrorists designed to bring about the disintegration of organized society. In a sense, the whole of society is the victim of terrorist extortion. In essence, this type of extortion is an attack upon the will of those whose values are affected in some way so as to cause them to surrender a material or other advantage to those who have brought pressure to bear upon them. Its effects upon the mind are scarcely less troublesome than the material losses occasioned by it. *No one is immune from the crime of extortion.* It depends solely upon whether the terrorists can seize hold of an asset which is sufficiently important to cause those entitled to its enjoyment to surrender something of value to the terrorists in order to conserve some other value. Extortion is a crime capable of assuming many forms and is consistently practiced by ordinary criminals. It is the stock-in-trade of organized crime.[5] It is a peculiarly insidious crime, designed to make those who are victims of it weaker—mentally, morally, and materially—and those who seek to profit by it stronger.

The crime of extortion, whatever its form and whether it be terroristic or otherwise, invariably produces important value dilemmas for those who are subjected to it. These are not merely of a philosophical character but have their practical aspects as well. It is as well to give some preliminary thought to these in the planning of protective responses. It is sometimes laid down as a general proposition that there should never be a surrender to blackmail. This postulate is usually pronounced quite categorically, without reservations. This advice is based, in the main, on a sound, common sense rule, that once having given in to a blackmailer, he will be encouraged to continue his depredations until the victim is bled white. The blackmailer is never satisfied; his criminal appetite is not appeased by a single success. This proposition is amply demonstrated by numerous criminal cases on the point. Common experience is a sound guide in this area. It is thus deduced, as a general rule of conduct, that a person who is blackmailed should resist from the start the attempt to extort anything of value from him and should cooperate fully with the authorities in bringing the blackmailer to justice. The blackmailer, like the hostage-taker, places himself in a very exposed position. This is, obviously, a satisfactory rule in a limited context. While the person being blackmailed may well suffer shame or embarassment in consequence of his firmness, the end result will be to his advantage. His material losses, as well as his mental anguish, are likely to be lessened by cooperation with the authorities.

The limitations of this advice should clearly be understood by those who offer it. There are those who would extend this advice, without too great a discrimination, to situations covering terroristic extortion. Indeed, official United States policy regarding kidnapping and hostage taking has been predicated upon it since 1972.[6] This advice, though in accord with much policy that is suggested, both at home and abroad, is not one which can be universally adhered to with confidence. Fear of "giving in" to the extortionist tends to cloud the judgment and obscure the issues. In fact, there are important distinctions to observe. Primarily, in the case of terroristic extortion, the victims do not enjoy the measure of protection from the legal system that is accorded the blackmail victim. The balance of power, and, accordingly, the extent of the interests at risk, are different. In the ordinary criminal case, society *can* help the victim if he will cooperate with the authorities; he suffers a lesser harm as a result of his refusal to give in to the blackmailer's demands. Such considerations do not obtain in the case of terrorist blackmail. Society, as a whole, may gain from firmness; the individual interest may have to be sacrificed to the greater good. Hence, the value dilemma.

The extortion in terroristic cases will involve the lives and interests of many persons beyond the actual target of the extortion. Such firmness as is advocated with the criminal blackmailer, where the only victim is the individual directly blackmailed, cannot prevail over the lives and interests of many other persons. If such sacrifices are demanded of individuals for the good of society, generally, they must rest on other grounds. While the practical rule designed to deter the ordinary criminal extortionist, by denying him the fruits of his crime, may well seem to be a vaulable one, this must always be weighed against the actual suffering produced in third-party victims and society as a whole where a terrorist situtation is created. Such evaluations must be made as dispassionately as possible. This is crucially illustrated in the kidnapping, hostage taking and skyjacking situations, where the pressure of extortion is placed upon private individuals or governments to surrender some asset of value to the terrorists in return for the safety of the victims whose lives have been placed in jeopardy. Very often, what is demanded produces an acute conflict of interest, because its surrender to some might seem unimportant, while to others it is fundamental. In the abstract, it may always be possible to resist extortion. It may even be good policy to advocate in advance that this be done. Yet such advice makes it extremely hard for those who have to bargain. Excruciating decisions have to be taken when human lives are at stake in consequence of a desire to maintain principles. Difficulties are compounded when the bases of those principles are not clear or sufficiently well understood. A definite understanding of priorities is needed. If the terrorist can set up a situation where he is able to force those with whom he is dealing not merely to accede to his demands but to surrender their declared principles as well, he has secured a double victory. As a general rule, if the value of human life is regarded sufficiently highly, it will always be very hard not to give in to any type of extortion when this life is realistically threatened by terrorist action. Where the particular life in question is deemed to hold some singular importance, all other interests are likely to be subordinated to its preservation.

In a practical sense, the crime of extortion is really a matter of power. Its success or failure depends on the extent to which the terrorist can bring pressure to bear so as to override the principles and countermeasures that can be developed to contain it. Where a persistent or extended terrorist campaign is concerned, policy decisions will have had to be taken at the highest government level. The surrender of human life to the maintenance of a principle of governmental policy may well be deemed necessary though regrettable.[7] There may well come a time, in any country and in any society, when the sacrifice of human life and property interests has to be prudently considered in the wider context of preserving some form of organized society against the terrorist menace. Where this extreme condition occurs, the sacrifice of an individual human life must be seen as part of the larger price that must be paid to preserve other lives from almost certain destruction by terrorists. From the perspective of individual protection, it is as well to determine in advance where such policies and priorities currently exist so as to be able to allow for them in the event of terrorist extortion occurring. Those exposed to situations in which no bargaining with terrorists is possible are entitled to know the hazards in advance.[8]

NOTES

1. Mario Puzo, *The Godfather* (Greenwich, Conn.: Fawcett Crest, 1969), p. 213.
2. See, on this, Maria Esther Gilio, *The Tupamaro Guerillas* (New York: Saturday Review Press, 1972).
3. MacDonald reports on an ingenious time bombing scheme in 1971 where the writer of letters to the media stated his intention to use the bombs "to kidnap property and offer it in exchange for the freedom of our people." John M. MacDonald, *Bombers and Firesetters,* p. 19.
4. Ransoms of over 60 million dollars are reported to have been collected by Argentinian terrorists.
5. See, on this, Mark H. Furstenburg, "Violence and Organized Crime," in *Crimes of Violence,* Staff Report to the National Commission on the Causes and Prevention of Violence, Vol. 13 (Washington, D.C.: U.S. Government Printing Office, 1969), pp. 911-939.

6. See *Political Kidnappings, 1968-1973,* A Staff Study Prepared by the Committee on Internal Security, United States House of Representatives (Washington, D.C.: U.S. Government Printing Office, 1973), p. 8.
7. The Israelis, in particular, have felt that any concessions to, or even dealings with, terrorists would irreparably imperil the national security; and this principle has been upheld even under the most difficult of circumstances, such as those resulting in the deaths of twenty-one Israeli schoolchildren at Maalot on May 15, 1975.
8. This is particularly the case where government employees are concerned and in some especially hazardous situations, such as those prevailing in correctional institutions.

Terrorist Profiles

"Once upon a time, not very long ago, the term 'terrorist' was tolerably clear to most people, mostly because terrorists told us who they were and what they were doing. In the Nineteenth Century, for example, anarchists proudly called themselves terrorists, traced their lineage at least back to the French Revolution, and sometimes to the Order of Assassins in Medieval Islam. Later, Trotsky was not embarrassed to speak of the benefits of the Red Terror. The last group to describe itself as a terrorist organization was the one widely known as 'The Stern Gang' thirty years ago. Today, the term has so many abusive connotations that no terrorist will ever call himself one publicly, and he will make every effort to pin that term on his enemy."

David Rapoport[1]

The Terrorist Profile

As was indicated, it is extremely difficult to provide a simple, all-embracing definition of terrorism. It is unlikely that this difficulty will be overcome in the foreseeable future. As might be anticipated, therefore, it is even more difficult to construct a relatively simple profile of those who engage in this very complex, violent activity.[2] This was the case with the well-known "skyjacker profile." While it is always a useful adjunct to security procedures to have some means to identify in advance those against whom countermeasures should be taken, profiles of great simplicity, though attractive, are relatively worthless. Generalizations serve only as a basis for discussion, not action. What must be provided, rather, is a relatively sophisticated analysis of the principal characteristics and action patterns of those who engage in acts of terrorism so as to categorize or group them in a way that will permit adequate countermeasures being adapted to their individual case. While those various acts characterized as terrorism can be reduced, descriptively and analytically, to a relatively small number of tactics or techniques with a common basis for each, the diversity of those human beings who engage in this behavior defies any such simple categorization. Given the right combination of circumstances, almost anyone can become a terrorist of sorts. Nevertheless, some kind of taxonomy must be produced in order that a useful discussion, for protective security purposes, can be developed.

Many classifications of those who engage in different manifestations of terroristic behavior have been attempted. All classifications are really quite artificial and arbitrary. The National Advisory Committee Task Force on Disorders and Terrorism[3] made a useful distinction between "terrorists" and "quasi-terrorists," but this must be further refined for the purposes of setting up protective services. Dr. Frederick J. Hacker, a California psychiatrist, has, in his book of the same name, grouped terrorists into the three categories of Crusaders, Criminals, and Crazies.[4] This is, in some ways, a very useful categorization for it enables certain simple distinctions to be made even though some of the persons assigned to one group might well fit another. For the present purposes, a somewhat similar, tripartite categorization will be essayed so as to divide these subjects into: *organized terrorist groups, quasi-terrorists,* and *terroristic misfits.* Each of these categories presents its own distinctive problems from a security perspective and those who fit into these categories can generally be identified by fairly easily recognizable features.

In dealing practically with the problem of terrorism, and terrorists, there are two fundamental questions that must be posed. *Who are they?* and *What do they want?* What they have done might be all too painfully obvious, despite the problems in putting a name to it. What invariably remains to be clarified is *who* has done these terrible things and *why* they have done them. No countermeasures of any specificity can be developed until such time as these questions can be answered in relation to the case in hand. They can be answered, in a very preliminary fashion, by identifying those to whom they relate as being members of known organizations with fairly clearly defined objectives. It is characteristic of the group to provide anonymity for individuals while seeking a maximum of publicity for the collective endeavor. A large number of those characterized as terrorists can be placed in such groupings. The fact of association with a group in itself tells a great deal about the individual in question.

Organized Terrorist Groups

This category will comprise, basically, those groups of *political* terrorists that have emerged in a fairly well-defined form. Such groups, their structure and personnel, will usually be well known to law enforcement authorities.[5] Their activities, and at least their more prominent members, will have attracted media attention. Having regard to the definition of terrorism that has been adopted here, it will exclude those criminal organizations that, although using terroristic methods, have no clearly defined political objective. Such an exclusion is, it is stressed, quite arbitrary and, to some extent, unrealistic. It would, in strictness, exclude many of the Italian criminal gangs who are responsible for much of the kidnapping, currently, in various parts of Italy.[6] It would also exclude many of the same types of persons organized for very similar activities in Latin America. As has already been pointed out, the activities, organization,and territory of such groups is often shared with many of the true terrorist groups. The arbitrary character of this exclusion should be noted and, where appropriate, overriden by those concerned with the provision of protective services.

It has become the fashion of late to identify political terrorists by organizational names which tend to reflect some political ideology and very often the name of a dead martyr figure.[7] While this is convenient and somewhat attractive schematically for the purposes of writing about such groups and their characteristics, the idea of labeling in this way is sometimes of misleading value. There is a tendency to think of such named groups as being "identified" or "out in the open." This is far from being the case. *Terrorism is a clandestine activity.* Terrorists do not go around wearing labels identifying their affiliations after the fashion of delegates to a conference. Security considerations alone preclude such behavior. When such groups start wearing uniforms, or even armbands or other distinctive insignia, their operations have clearly entered another phase. Very often, the only purpose of a label or name of this sort is for the propaganda value it might have and for identification of the group with certain operations, such as bombings, for which they wish to take public responsibility. The idea of a label of this sort can be, at times, very misleading and give the impression that one is dealing with a much larger organization than is the case. The Symbionese Liberation Army, at the time when its activities constituted a serious law enforcement problem, was extremely small indeed; but the grandiloquent title assumed by its members and broadcast throughout the media gave the impression to the public that the group was larger, better organized, and much more formidable than it really was.[8]

There is now voluminous literature available from which the names of most active and inactive groups of organized terrorists can be extracted. Such an exercise may serve a useful purpose for the security specialist but, again, it is cautioned that too much attention should not be paid to these labels. Personnel and even objectives change quite rapidly, as witness the case with the West German terrorist groups. Groups, particularly small ones, engage in frequent metamorphoses like those to which Venceremos, the Symbionese Liberation Army, and the New World Liberation Front were subject. There is much ambivalence in this. These groups want the advantages of publicity yet none of the inconvenience of the accompanying identification.

Perhaps the most sensible division among organized political terrorist groups that can be made is into those groups that have some specifically declared territorial objective and those that do not. This is a very distinctive form of affiliation and tends to color the group's entire range of activities. Those associations that have an unalterable territorial affiliation, such as the

IRA, are now comparatively few among modern groups. They were much more common during the era of decolonization following 1945 when the great powers were in the process of reassessing their imperial commitments. Such groups generally have a realistic expectation of extending their terrorist activities into a full scale guerrilla war so as to be able to challenge the established authorities ruling the territory to which they lay claim, with a view to eventually assuming a genuine governmental role. For such groups, terrorism is not engaged in for its own sake, but is strictly a disagreeable means to an earnestly desired end. This was the standard pattern of terrorism from 1945 onwards as the big colonial powers relinquished their jurisdictions over the territories that they controlled, and those territories themselves began to fall to a power struggle among the indigenous groups. Terrorist groups came and went with remarkable rapidity as the power struggles were resolved, and the victors settled down to an uneasy legitimacy with the strongest desire to bury their unsavory past. Much of today's terroristic rhetoric for all groups is born out of these wars of national liberation, such as those for Algeria, Aden, and Cyprus, where terrorism became a tactic or technique utilized against the foreign oppressor by certain groups that were unable to organize resistance in any other realistic way. Terrorism was a product of weakness, of moral and material inferiority. It is widely regarded as a necessary, if regrettable, step on the road to legitimacy. Such terrorists were, indeed, irregular soldiers fighting by terroristic means a vastly superior regular army. Eventually they emerged, much like the World War II Partizans, with all the trappings of military organization; sometimes, indeed, like the Irgun, becoming the nucleus of the army of the new state.[9] Terrorism took on, therefore, a heroic quality and became identified with patriotism and the interests of the people. This sentiment has never really been lost and has been capitalized on by modern, nonterritorial groups, often in a most inappropriate fashion.

As the world settled down, and fewer and fewer overseas territories remained under the direct control of the big powers, the pattern of terroristic activity began to change. There was less emphasis on territory and more on ideology. A relatively few, real trouble spots of the former sort, among them Northern Ireland and the Middle East, remained. These continued to generate much of the "old style" terrorism. Nevertheless, the tactics and techniques learned in those earlier struggles began to filter down to smaller power groups having a less direct association with the struggle for liberty in their particular national territories; and whose actions began to take on a much more diffuse character. There are now, accordingly, comparatively few terrorist groups that are *solely* concerned with the power struggle inside a single territory and are only engaged, as are, for example the black terrorists in Southern Africa, in seeking to dislodge, within a restricted territorial area, the established government of a particular country, the legality of which they challenge by these means. The majority of political terrorists in the world today, although identified with the aspirations, techniques, motivations and history of the earlier nationalistic terroristic groups, have but slight relationship to them. They can only properly be described as their successors in an ideological sense. These "new" groups are not concerned with the immediate conversion of their own illicit activities into legitimate political power. Their relationship to the social, political and economic structure of the country with which they are most closely associated is generally much more tenuous and less realistic than that of their ideological forebears. Their aims are less concrete or as well defined as the terrorists of yesteryear.

True, territorially aligned political terrorist groups have, generally, certain fairly well-defined characteristics. While their composition, philosophies and methods vary greatly, they have much in common—even in their extreme forms—so that much that could be said of the Stern Gang would be equally applicable to, say, the Provisional Wing of the IRA. Their energies are concentrated against a specific target; namely, the representatives of the country seen as being the oppressor. This does not rule out the possibility of innocents being victimized, but it does tend to limit the scope and nature of the struggle. Nor does it rule out collaboration—moral, material or technological— with other groups.

In the case of a colonial power, the activities of such groups are mainly directed at the military and police forces of the dominant country and against civilian representatives and nationals of that country occupying responsible positions or visiting in some way, as tourists. The objective is to force a reappraisal of relations through fear, the theory being that, if the cost of remaining is perceived as being too high, control will be surrendered and the "oppression" will cease. Where there is an internal or domestic power struggle in progress, all the legitimate representatives of the established government are regarded as fair targets of the terrorist groups. Those in authority are particularly vulnerable. The activities of these groups are generally, therefore, restricted to a fairly well-defined area; namely, the territory controlled by those who are regarded as the enemy. The hated targets are generally to be found within that area and, for a variety of reasons, not the least of which is the propaganda value of the operation, will be struck at within that area. This means, in general, that the majority of operations of such groups will not spill over into the international arena and will only affect persons of other nationalities in a somewhat indirect way. The history of the operations of the IRA—of both the Official and Provisional Wings—exemplifies this.[10] While observation of this was substantially true in the case of all original, territorially aligned groups that were seeking to throw off the yoke of the "imperialist oppressor," this cannot be accounted strictly true of today's "new" terrorists for a number of fairly obvious reasons. Even though they retain their fundamental territorial allegiance and aims, they no longer feel the need for restricting themselves in terms of action. The ambit of the struggle has widened, international relations have become a major target, modern communications have substantially changed the perspectives for offensive action and, in general, the potential arena of the struggle has been greatly enlarged.

These old-style territorially aligned terrorists have, in effect, become merged with a new breed of international terrorists whose objectives and ambit of activity have become truly transnational. The battleground has become the world, rather than a single country, although the ultimate objective might still be domination of a particular national territory. *Terrorism now knows no frontiers.* It may strike wherever and whenever it is considered to serve the purposes of those who employ it. This new breed of *transnational terrorism* is deserving of the closest study, for the term covers a multitude of sins.[11]

The transnational terrorist is simply one who is prepared to operate in his own cause, or any other, on any territory, and against any target, wherever and whenever it might seem appropriate for his purposes. Old and new terrorists share a common view of the possibilities inherent in such a strategy. Thus it could come about that the IRA—the declared interest and aim of which lies in promoting the establishment of a united Ireland in which they and their adherents would have a substantial governing voice—might extend the struggle to engage British targets in other parts of the world having no necessary connection with the territory in dispute. The principal, territorial aim would remain as before. The objective would be simply to weaken the interests, power and influence of the British enemy wherever such interests are to be found, on the theory that whatever weakens the enemy anywhere can only serve to weaken, in turn, his hold over the disputed territory. There are many obvious ways in which such an altered, transnational strategy would be put into effect. Thus, members of the IRA might engage in the assassination of British businessmen in Latin America, the blowing up of British airliners anywhere in the world, the kidnapping of British officials in various European countries or any other activities on a worldwide scale. The countries, where these activities took place would obviously be alarmed and inconvenienced. The terrorists' hope is that it would cause them to reevaluate their relations with the United Kingdom and that this, in turn, would have an impact upon British policy with regard to Ireland. The fact that, in the main, they have not widened their activities much beyond the British Isles is not an ideological or dogmatic postulate, but simply that, in the present state of the struggle and having regard to the nature of their own organization and resources, they have not seen a value in undertaking a worldwide engagement of this type. Although the Irish example has been chosen here, the point would fit equally any of a number of other groups and their perceived antagonists.

Many of the territorially aligned groups have, indeed, in the last few years, extended their operations in this transnational fashion. The most important example, perhaps, is that of the various Palestinian liberation groups that have felt themselves forced to resort to terrorism.[12] These groups have struck in many parts of the world, not only against specific Israeli targets, but against targets more properly associated with other countries with a view to pressuring those nations to adopt a certain stand in favor of their own movements or against the state of Israel. These groups have also struck extensively at international aviation interests and have not limited themselves in any way to a close identification with the territorial interests that they are seeking to espouse. All who dealt with Israel in any way were regarded as fair game. Nevertheless, regardless of their tactics, their interests remain clearly indentifiable with a single cause, and while they are supported and maintained by a diversity of interest groups, their objective remains the liberation of what they claim to be their own national territory. Like their Jewish predecessors, terrorism is simply a disagreeable means to a desired end. Their terrorism, like that of the Jews, would doubtless cease on attainment of their territorial objective. Their *modus operandi* is transnational, but their objective remains strictly limited and territorial. Their association with other individuals and groups should not be allowed to obscure that fact.

An entirely different type of group now presents itself for study. These groups are quite different from those already considered. These are truly transnational groups that have no territorial ambitions of their own whatsoever, nor any firm affiliation with groups having such a territorial ambition. Loose in structure and ideals, they may operate anywhere and on almost any account. These groups, which are often multiracial, are characterized mainly by their adherence to vague principles of a nihilistic character embracing a grandiose ideal of "world revolution" and a body of dogma transcending purely territorial and ideological aims. Such groups often have quite bizarre objectives and equally strange sounding names. Some members of these groups are little more than international mercenaries, ready to serve any cause at a price. There is, clearly, no shortage of causes. There has been, particularly since the Arab oil embargo and the dramatic increase of oil revenues, no shortage of funding for such terroristic enterprises. Some of these groups, such as the Japanese Red Army, have, although enjoying a national identification, a worldwide concept of their role that permits them to operate on account of a variety of causes that have only the most tenuous links with each other. Japanese terrorists were responsible for the massacre of Christian pilgrims at Lod Airport in May 1973, ostensibly in support of the Palestinian cause. George Habash, leader of the PFLP, has had numerous contacts with Japanese terrorists. On a close examination, there are comparatively few of these nihilistic groups. Most of the transnational terrorists are genuinely aligned with a national or territorial movement, or comprise foreign nationals who are working individually with such a group, or who have an alliance of interests that makes for a truly international approach to the question or cause that they are supporting. Many of these international operations have been mounted in recent years and the so-called "Carlos" group is a prime example of this type of transnational terrorism with international participation.[13] Such groups are often covertly financed and supported by interested nation states.

Many of these modern international or transnational groups are interrelated in some significant way. Sometimes they will be related by sharing common objectives and a common ideology. This is particularly the case with Leftist groups and those professing an anti-capitalist, anti-imperialist philosophy. Terrorists, generally, share a common literature. At other times, they will be related by a reliance upon a common source of financing or a common supplier of arms.[14] At other times, the groups' identities will be even more closely related by reason of having shared common operational experiences or having trained together. There is evidence of a certain amount of technology transfer among the groups. During the earlier period of activity of the Palestinian movements, many groups from all over the world took advantage of their training facilities in The Lebanon, Jordan and Syria. The original members of the BaaderMeinhof group trained in these facilities. These camps welcomed serious proponents of terrorism from different parts of the world and made available the experience of the Palestinian terrorists in a very intensive fashion. This was not an entirely disinterested gesture. Following the termination of the Lebanese Civil War and the elimination of the guerrilla camps in Jordan, the South Yemen became a base for the training of international groups that were supplemented from time-to-time by released "comrades" who had been flown to that country as a result of being granted asylum.

The nonterritorially aligned terrorist groups—the true transnational terrorists—may well have a definite territorial base of operations and a preponderance of members of one nationality among their ranks. This is the case with the German groups that have operated under various names since 1968, as well as the Japanese groups that have engaged in terroristic enterprises throughout the world.[15] These groups comprise a small core cadre that has operated out of Germany and Japan respectively. Such groups maintain a fairly loose relationship with other groups around the world, and their main point of commonality is in their generally nihilistic or anarchistic philosophy. They are quite distinct in one respect from territorially oriented groups. Although comprising a majority of members of some particular nationality, they have no real prospect of altering the political situation in their own country so significantly as to be able to ascend to power. They have no expectations of immediate or even eventual legitimacy. Their aspirations are, therefore, attuned to the causing of massive, worldwide disruption in the hope that their ultimate objective of changing the world power structure and ideology will be realized out of the resultant chaos. The magnitude of these aspirations is matched by the grandiose nature of their terroristic operations. Such groups tend to have no fixed base of operations and move with relative ease across frontiers using false documentation, ample funds, and a formidable arsenal of weaponry. Their organization is very flexible and recruitment tightly controlled. They pose a particular problem for law enforcement in countries like those in Europe where the tendency has been for a lessening of frontier restrictions over the years and a greater liberality in travel and commerce. These factors greatly favored the West German terrorist groups that were able to operate against German targets from the Netherlands, France, and Austria with relative impunity until recently. Such groups very often enjoy covert material and financial support from countries which like to claim that they espouse a "revolutionary" philosophy and have aims loosely tied to those of various ill-formed liberation movements throughout the world. Many of the most horrifying and spectacular terroristic exploits of recent years are attributable to these goups. *They do not risk losing broadbased public support.*

The organizational structure of all these terrorist groups is designed in some way or another to prevent the gathering of intelligence about them and to prevent their being infiltrated by counterintelligence operatives. Whether these groups are organized in tight "no contact" cells, or whether they have some other organizational structure, there is always the intention to insulate the higher echelons and those having the directive capacity of the organization from those who are engaged with purely operational matters. This, again, tells something of the character of those who engage in these activities. Many of the territorially aligned groups, and those that aspire to the attainment of a position of political legitimacy in the not too distant future, will have an "above ground" or recognized political branch. This may have already emerged in a definite fashion, as for example the PLO, or will be in the course of emergence, such as is the case of some of the African groups engaged in their struggle for liberation of Southern Africa. The apparently benign and conciliatory character of some of these emergent political groups should not blind one to the vicious nature of the underground operatives who are still engaged in propagating terroristic tactics and principles while being shielded from the consequences of their action by the political wing or arm of their organization. Like old soldiers, "old" terrorists never die; they either attain political legitimacy or simply fade away. The links between the two arms of the movement might be extremely unclear and even denied publicly by the leadership, as was the case with Al Fatah and Black September. Nevertheless, these connections must always be realistically taken into account when assessing the prospects for terrorism in any particular area and at any particular time, and in determining what countermeasures might be productive against it.

All organized terrorist movements are hierarchical in character. They have a definite command structure, a division of responsibilities, and people are assigned their role with regard to the internal politics and power structure of the organization. They represent a microcosm of regular, politically organized societies. This is very important for any classification of terrorists and the creation of anything in the nature of a terrorist profile. Some terrorists will be high on the organizational ladder while others will not. Terrorist movements, like antiestablishment cultures, generally have no shortage of recruits at the lower level, particularly those movements that are Marxist-oriented and especially in times of considerable world instability or crisis. Foot soldiers of this order are rarely difficult to find. Such persons will show wide variations by age, sex, occupation, race, religion, and other characteristics, but their common feature lies in their willingness to serve, fanatically, in the most violent and dangerous of situations, a cause which is all too often unclear and not perfectly understood by them. These "foot soliders" are not simply moronic. Many of these lower level operatives will be quite intelligent, from good homes and family backgrounds, well educated, and often extremely idealistic. They are apt to remain somewhat anonymous in character and, if they operate for long enough, tend to take on the character and style of the group, within which their own personalities and natures become submerged. A number of these lower level operatives are personally committed to the espousal of various left-wing doctrines of an extreme kind although the actual extent of their knowledge about social and political theory will vary from case to case. While it is important to see them as members of a group and to understand how the group ethic acts upon them and their personalities, it is even more important to study them as individuals in order to be able to understand their propensities and to develop effective countermeasures against them.[16]

From a response perspective, the importance of fixing the individual in the hierarchy, as well as determining the group to which he belongs, is of the utmost importance. The "who" of terrorism can only receive a satisfactory answer through such a study. The degree of determination with which the terrorist will press home his assignement, the possibility of bargaining with him or mitigating the harm which he seeks to cause, will depend to a very large extent on his personal psychology as well as the degree of his commitment to a cause or an organization. *Organizations dispose; individuals execute.*

The hand that pulls the trigger or places the bomb is usually far removed from the mind that has developed and ordered the operation. Those who are in executive control of operations for organized terrorist groups are rarely personally involved in a way that might lead to their death or capture.[17] It is a sign of aberration or primitive organization where the reverse is the case. Terrorists have long since learned that their directive capacities should be isolated or insulated from the active confrontation phase of their operation so as to maintain their command structure intact. Terrorist generals do not go into battle with their troops. In some of the more spectacular operations, control of the undertaking has been maintained from a considerable distance, making full use of modern communications.[18] In some cases, the directive leadership has even been in another country from that in which the actual operation itself is taking place. Many terrorist operations in Europe and Africa have been directed from Beirut and Damascus. Such an arrangement greatly enhances the terrorist's bargaining power and improves his prospects of increasing the pressure to a point where those subject to his attacks might be prepared to accede to his demands. It is axiomatic that a leader should not take part in a "confrontation style" operation where a likely outcome is his death or capture by the authorities. To do so is a sign of inexperience or naivete'.[19]

While the identities of many of the key leaders of transnational terrorist groups, as well as those having a more specific territorial alignment, are known to security forces and intelligence networks throughout the world, they are often well protected and reasonably secure in the safe havens they have made for themselves. Their own protective security arrangements offer instructive lessons in security. Only on very rare occasions have persons of these upper echelons been subject to attack by security forces, notably the Israelis and West Germans. By and large, the unwritten rule is observed that "generals do not shoot generals." As in the case of organized crime, it is generally those of the middle echelons of executive range or management that are taken prisoner and dealt with according to law. There have been some exceptions in Latin America, notably Raul Sendic, the Tupamaro leader, and Roberto Santucho, the ERP leader in Argentina. Following the deaths of the Israeli athletes in Munich in 1972, a wide ranging campaign to trace operatives at all levels of the various Palestinian terrorist movements throughout the world was launched. The overt operations in which the two sides engaged were paralleled by other covert operations which in a number of cases led to attacks upon higher echelon members of the Palestinian terrorist groups, notably in Paris and Beirut. Some died in car bombings, while others were shot down in intimidatory fashion by government operatives. Exceptional situations call for exceptional measures and, in general, the upper echelons of terrorist movements have all tended to be less accessible as a result of the experience of this time. Certainly, those such as George Habash and Wadi Haddad, who have become notorious for their directive exploits and who are aware of the danger that these create for them, take great personal care to avoid being ensnared by the security forces of the opposite side. Terrorist leaders are difficult subjects to study—at least until such time as they feel able to make a safe transformation to a more respectable status.

With respect to organized groups, something must be said here about the relatively new phenomenon of the emergence of the woman terrorist.[20] These "new" women terrorists are invariably group oriented; however individualistic their drives and motivations, they tend to function as members of a group. This has been a quite alarming development in recent years. Women have long been associated with idealistic, organized terrorist movements, but usually their position has been of a somewhat subordinate character, and they have been employed in positions of a noncombative nature or those in which the advantages of their sex allowed them to carry out an operation more effectively than would have been the case for a man. *We are now seeing the woman terrorist emerging in dominant numbers in some groups and in a directive capacity in others.* In some of the European terrorist organizations, such as the Baader-Meinhof group and the Red Cells in Germany, women have actually been in a majority and have been personally responsible for some of the more vicious acts of terrorism that have been committed by these groups. Even in Italian and Latin American groups women have come to take a dominant operational role. The aggressiveness and independence of some of these women operatives have been quite notable. In some cases, women such as the skyjacker Leila Khalid and the Japanese terrorist Fusako Shigenobu have achieved an international prominence, although the publicity surrounding them is probably greater than their actual participation in terroristic activities would warrant. Certainly other women have now surpassed them in viciousness and commitment to terrorism.

The emergent role of women in terrorist groups poses a very serious threat to the security of individuals whose lives and other interests might be threatened by terrorist groups, and special problems for law enforcement and private security agencies. A thorough study of this subject, in depth, is requisite before any protective measures can be undertaken. Some subjects will be in greater danger from the female terrorist than others. The delicate male/female relationship is one which is peculiarly prone to exploitation by clandestine groups and which carries evident dangers within itself that threaten the security of the individual in a very significant way. Young, seemingly innocent girls are rarely regarded as a threat by grown men. Suffice it to say that the West German banker Ponto was shot dead on his own doorstep by a young female friend of the family, and an Argentinian police chief was blown up by a bomb placed under his bed by a teenage girl friend of his daughter. A much greater understanding of the modern female terrorist is needed before anything in the nature of an effective profile can be developed. Physical as well as psychological characteristics show wide variations. Biographical materials suggest that sexual factors may be extremely significant. It certainly takes more than an ordinary degree of anger, hostility or disappointment to turn a woman into a terrorist. The motive is usually an intensely personal one, unique to the individual concerned. For the moment, it is necessary to identify those groups that employ significant numbers of female terrorists or which have female terrorists in a directive capacity. It is better from a security perspective to approach the problem through the group than through the individual.

The fact that an operative belongs to an identifiable terrorist group says little, as such, about him as an individual. It is, however, a good starting point for a case study or the gathering of intelligence. Some terrorist groups evolve out of other political associations, going "underground" so to speak,[21] while others represent an original creation. Some members will have known each other over a relatively long period before embarking on terroristic activity, while others will have been recruited only for a specific operation. Some terrorist groups restrict their recruitment to persons of a particular nationality or religion, while others are concerned more with a person's ideological commitments. The depth of these usually has to be taken on trust, but it is usual in many terrorist groups to force the new recruit to undertake some violent act, a killing or bombing, so as to reinforce his commitment in a practical, irrevocable way. Generally speaking, the level of ideological commitment will be in some way or another correlated with the position of responsibility and the nature of the mission undertaken by the operative. Some missions necessarily require a fanatical attachment to the organization and its ideals. The leadership of organized groups may well regard many of their lower operatives as being relatively expendable. Some terrorists will have specific indoctrination along these lines.[22] This means that they may be chosen for their willingness to engage in what amounts, virtually, to suicide missions. It is always necessary to know, from a response perspective, whether this willingness stems from indoctrination, a fanatical commitment to the cause, or, primarily, from a patent or latent mental instability. None of these conditions is necessarily exclusive of the others. The nature of the political struggle in which the organization is engaged may determine whether this commitment to terrorism at all costs stems from conviction or faith in the political objective of the organization, or whether it is attributable more to a psychosis or lack of intelligence on the part of the individual operative. In the final analysis, only the study of the individual can reveal the true source of his dedication.

The number of highly skilled terrorists operating in any one area at any one time is usually extemely small, and the groups themselves tend to be comprised of the dedicated, hard-core cadre with a number of relatively peripheral followers. These latter are extremely important, for while they may not themselves engage in acts of violence, they provide the logistical support, services, and safe havens that make terrorism possible. The Tupamaros are an example of a group having a hard-core band of dedicated operatives supported in varying degrees by sympathizers dispersed throughout the community. The West German Terrorists, never numerous—although reports as to their actual numbers varied—had, at one time, similar, wide-ranging support in the community. The overall political, social and economic context in which such groups operate also tends to have its effect on the nature of the operations and the character and qualities of those who are engaged in undertaking them. Generally speaking, the larger the group, the more unwieldy it becomes, the more prone to schismatic conflicts, and the more susceptible to penetration by counterintelligence operations.

So far as organized terrorist groups are concerned, useful profiles can be drawn up either on a collective basis, or on an individual basis. There should be maintained, for each relatively well-defined and known entity, a collective profile which indicates the group's ideology, its apparent objectives, its methods and techinique, its organizational structure, its geographical identification (if appropriate), its numerical strength, and its track record. This will be instructive with regard to any dealing which might be necessary with the group as a whole. It is especially necessary as a starting point for any threat assessment exercise. Such a profile tends to give a representative notion of the group and those associated with it and provides a rough and ready guide for estimating its potentialities in any particular situation. It is only as good as the data on which it is based. It should be constantly reviewed in the light of further and better information. To a certain extent, the profile of the collective body will give at least some indication of the profiles of the individual participants in it. Well-established groups tend to choose persons according to a fairly consistent criteria, and the pattern imposed by the organization tends to reflect in the personalities, attitudes, and capabilities of the individuals. The longer a group is in existence, the more evident becomes the "group ethic"; the IRA is a good example. After a while, however, splinter groups may form, and these might differ radically from their parent body.

It is only possible to construct useful individual terrorist profiles from known terrorists, and this information will only be reliable if it is obtained with relation to terrorists who have been clearly identified or apprehended in the course of some operation. For obvious reasons, it is not easy to study active, "working" terrorists. Studies based upon the lives and careers of former terrorists can be misleading.[23] Such studies are anachronistic; times change and so do styles. It is generally unsafe to extrapolate from individual profiles so as to develop a general profile, as there may well be marked variations even within one particular organization. *There is no such thing as a "typical terorrist."* Any profile designed with such an ambitious purpose in mind is quite useless. In particualr, the degree of mental stability of individual terrorists will vary quite widely. This is of the highest importance to those designing protective measures. The individuals still remain largely as individuals notwithstanding that they are participating in a group activity. They are, accordingly, subject to all the peculiarities of their own consititutional make-up. It is the *effect* of the group upon the individual that is important. Wide, general profiles can be extremely misleading to those engaged in providing protective services. They can give a false sense of security. Profiles that purport to be based on general factors of education, age, sex, and social class are often very inaccurate. An unreliable profile can do more harm than good. *This is an area where, particularly, there is no substitute for sound intelligence and the accurate, painstaking collection of information about individuals.* Only in this way can an individual profile of value be constructed. Whenever possible, photographs of individual terrorists should be obtained, and these must be constantly updated as terrorists frequently change their physical appearance to avoid being recognized.[24] This is especially true of terrorist leaders. *The importance of seeing terrorists as individuals and understanding their individual motivations and proclivities cannot be overstressed.*

Terrorism, while it is often a group phenomenon, is generally constructed largely out of individual drives and aspirations. It is only when these are thoroughly understood that a reasonable appraisal of the dangers from which the target figure might need protection can be reasonably accurately assessed. *Groups, as such, do not choose targets; individuals in groups do.* Knowing the individual is a first step to knowing the target likely to be chosen and the degree of risk to which it is exposed.

It is obviously a controversial matter to determine to what degree those participating in terroristic activity within the organized political groups might be regarded as mentally disturbed individuals. There are those who would argue that only madness can be the explanation for some of the awful deeds committed by terrorists. This is too sweeping and general to be of value. It depends, to a very large extent, where the line with regard to mental abnormality is to be drawn. The ordinary criteria for the measurement of mental health may well need some modification in this area. The standard against which persons might be measured is, obviously, not a fixed one; but it is evident that the soul-destroying, fearful work in which they are engaged requires a quite extraordinary insulation from the elements that comprise ordinary humanity. However much language may be bent to accommodate ideology, these are not ordinary soldiers fighting for a righteous cause. In order to be able to kill ruthlessly for a cause, under circumstances that allow of very little discrimination requires an unusual amount of hostility or hatred within the individual concerned, plus a somewhat curious distortion of his ordinary human sentiments, or else is the product of a distinctly abnormal personality.[25] Those who can do the deed with their own hands must be distinguished from those who only plan and prepare or offer aid and comfort. Some deeds look less terrible at a distance. In general, the biographies of known terrorists tend to suggest a marked streak of abnormality in most of them, and they become even more distorted and warped as a result of the activities that they undertake. Having killed once, they are more likely to do so again. In some, a process of denial operates so as to insulate them from their deeds. For others, commitment to violence is simply a road from which there is no turning back. Some terrorists will be markedly more vicious or inhuman than others, and these will be almost certainly suffering from some abnormality of the mind or some constitutional instability that is worthy of careful study. It is especially important to make an early identification of such individuals in cases of, for example, multiple hostage takings, as their behavior is likely to present an extraordinary danger to those in their power.[26] They may, thus, need to be marked out for special attention by the responding authorities.

In general, organized terrorist groups tend to pick their members from persons who do not exhibit any obvious degree of mental illness and certainly try to avoid persons who would be

ordinarily classed as psychotic. It should be borne in mind, however, that the symptoms of hysteria or paranoia that would alert
a trained mental health practitioner might well escape the notice
of those to whom they are but a "normal" facet of behavior. A little "wildness" or bizarre behavior can easily be overlooked if
other desirable qualities seem to be present. The Japanese,
Kozo Okamoto, captured at Lod Airport, is an example.[27] It is
equally certain that organized terrorist groups tend to number
among their ranks large numbers of persons who would properly be classified as psychopathic or sociopathic, These persons tend to be very unstable, difficult to control, and are often
capable of great violence. Provided they are regarded as expendable, the advantages of employing them might well be considered to outweigh the disadvantages. Unquestionably, the
mental condition of terrorists is a subject worthy of the closest
study, but comparatively little has been done even on those who
have been reduced into captivity. While some information—
usually second or third hand— can be obtained concerning the
mental state of active terrorists, they can only be properly studied after apprehension, and there are many obstacles to be
overcome before the process can be started. The career of the
individual terrorist is generally not a long one. Active terrorists
often die young. For this reason alone, the subject does not
present itself for study in a convenient form. Clinical accuracy in
the profiling of the individual terrorist is not to be expected. Perhaps the only, somewhat superficial, caution that need be
offered here, is reflection upon the fact that assignment of an
individual to the group denominated here as "organized terrorists" speaks in no way to the mental condition of the person in
question. The categories established here are quite arbitrary
and sometimes overlapping. The political motivation, or association with a political group, may be little more than a rationalization of an inward propensity or lust for violence for its own sake.
The group label is hardly more than a convenience for descrip-
tive or analytical purposes.

Quasi-terrorists[28]

These are loose organizations of persons or, more usually,
individuals who engage in terroristic acts in imitation of those
committed by politically organized groups rather than with any
specific terroristic purpose of their own. The acts themselves—

bombings, skyjackings, hostage takings—are often indistinguishable in form from those perpetrated by the first group. It is the
form alone, however, that is preserved. It is not so much what is
done as why it was done that reveals the difference. It is the tactic or technique that is utilized, often for purposes that have little
to do with the objectives for which terrorism is generated by
organized groups. The quasi-terrorist has seen something
occur that appears to produce a certain result. He, accordingly,
adapts it for his own purposes. The activities of those who par-
ticipate in undertakings of this sort are no less terrifying to their
victims. The nature, quality, and level of the fear produced are
not a proper index or scale for judgement. However, the differences in objective as well as the character and personalities of
those involved require that these incidents be differentiated and
handled in a different way from those involving the terrorist
organziations which were earlier discussed. They may be no
less dangerous for the immediate victims, but the prospects for
their satisfactory resolution are usually better. Quasi-terrorism
is really a very broad, artificial category which embraces the
activities not only of those members of the criminal classes who
characteristically use terror for ordinary criminal purposes,
such as the Mafia,[29] but also persons of a much lower order in
criminal activity who make use of terroristic tactics on an opportunistic or occasional basis.

The terroristic technique of hostage taking has been frequently imitated by persons who could be conveniently classified as quasi-terrorists. Spectacular, widely reported events
involving political terrorists often give rise to imitative behavior
as though by contagion. Many incidents occurring in the United
States are of this character and, indeed, the bulk of the experience of law enforcement authorities in the handling of such
incidents comes from this class. Frustrated bank robbers who
are often caught in the act as a result of a swift law enforcement
response have learned, almost as a matter of course, to take
hostages in order to bargain their way out of the situation in
which their criminal activities have placed them. The technique
that they use is, superficially, very similar to that used by organized terrorist groups, but is rarely successful in gaining them
anything more than a momentary respite from capture. They
lack the requisite planning and preparation and have no organization outside the immediate scene of the action capable of
bringing additional, diversionary pressure to bear. Such activity

is entered into with scarcely any thought for its consequences, and the main protective response is one of containment and a patient search for alternatives while everything is done to prevent harm coming to the victims who have been seized. Time is rarely on the side of the quasi-terrorist; he does not have the resources to make use of it. In general, this technique of handling the quasi-terrorist, in these situations, is effective and one which has been brought, in the United States, to a high degree of perfection by many law enforcement agencies.[30] This success is, it must be cautioned, no indication of the prospects of success against organized terrorist groups, for the activities of these might well require different techniques and strategies from those developed to deal with quasi-terrorists.

The quasi-terrorist has usually no ideological commitment to a cause and is simply using what seems to have worked for organized groups by adapting it for his own purposes. The lack of preparation and the lack of ability to think through the situation carefully make for a very unstable situation in which the principal object is to ensure that the perpetrator does nothing harmful as a result of panic or a false move. Those responding to a situation caused by a quasi-terrorist must be prepared to do much of his thinking for him.[31] They must be prepared to offer acceptable alternatives to those into which the perpetrator seems to have locked himself. The object, as always, is to try to ensure that the situation is brought to a rapid and satisfactory conclusion with a minimum of damage on any account. Because there is less commitment to a cause or an idea, more egotistical considerations generally prevail. Matters can usually be settled with the quasi-terrorist on the basis of what he is encouraged to see as his own self-interest.

Many skyjackings are of a quasi-terroristic character.[32] There is no political motivation at all in a majority of them, and the reason for the skyjacking is either an obscure, personal one stimulated by the desire to emulate what seems to have been effective in the case of organized political groups, or has a purely lucrative objective, as is the case where skyjacking is undertaken by common cirminals. The effect upon the response structure, as well as those who are victims in the skyjacking, is very similar to that which would be produced by terrorism of organized groups. The level of fear and the likelihood of death and destruction are no less real while the skyjacking is proceeding, but the patterns of handling such incidents are less involved, more direct, and suggestive of a more satisfactory outcome in the majority of cases. There are real dangers in responding to such incidents as though the perpetrators were organized political terrorists. This leads to overreaction and, often, to a violent outcome.[33] The quasi-terrorist as skyjacker is generally characterized by his lack of commitment to a cause and his singular application of the terroristic enterprise to the matter at hand. Although he may have a history of violent behavior, he is not a practitioner of violence for effect. He has no long-term objectives but is generally concerned with using terror for a very specific purpose which he may or may not repeat at a later date. The unfamiliarity of the skyjacker with his environment and the technicalities of the operation is usually very evident in these cases.

The diversity of quasi-terrorists and the wide range of possibilities that might give rise to activity on their part preclude any effective classification or the development of a useful profile. The Hanafi incident in Washington, D.C., in March 1977, although of an unusual, hybrid nature, is closer to a quasi-terroristic operation than any other.[34] The most that can be said of them is that those who are likely to act in similar situations have a tendency to respond to similar stimuli. Quasi-terrorism is a response motivated by fear; it is the response of the cornered rat.[35] While virtually every fleeing felon or frustrated bank robber will be different in character there will be certain commonalities about their responses to the type of situation in which they will seek to make use of terroristic tactical techniques. In their behavior, there is much rhetoric, empty bluff and braggadocio, but they can be dangerous if handled inappropriately. It is the emotional response to the stimulus that calls forth this activity from them that offers the best chance of classification for the purpose of developing an effective system of control. Few of these individuals, for example, despite the rhetoric that they use, are really as desperate as they seem to be. They are often inadequate personalities,[36] making the most of their brief moment in the spotlight. They are usually shallow and self-centered. They are overly anxious to preserve their own dignity and show they are firmly in control. Many of these individuals are bluffing and are certainly unwilling to risk their own lives. They are often quite well aware of the steps and procedures in the unfolding drama and follow them quite faithfully. In general, a patient, cautious evaluation of their behavior in the course of an incident is extremely revealing and is productive of sound results. Those concerned with the protection of the victim must be everything possible to lower the general climate of anxiety.

One situation that might usefully be classified as quasi-terrorist, although it differs somewhat from the conventional pattern of those examples that have been given, is the barricaded hostage situation within a jail, prison, or penitentiary. In these cases, the common terroristic features are present—the creation of massive fear, the development of a bargaining position—but quite often the actors have a higher degree of desperation than normal that will lead them to take greater risks and be less tender toward the life and physical integrity of their victims than would otherwise be the case. Especially in those jurisdictions where there is no death penalty, the hostage-takers may well feel that they have nothing to lose by killing their victims. These cases, such as occurred at Attica in 1971, are sometimes obscured by a plethora of political rhetoric, but they are different in nature and effect from the true political terrorist cases. While, to some extent, the present situation can be treated as falling within the quasi-hostage framework, there are special features about it that need to be distinguished and receive special study with regard to the design of adequate responses. Places where persons are kept in confinement, particularly if such individuals are dangerous and have, otherwise, no prospect of regaining their liberty, must have special security criteria applied to them.[37]

Terroristic Misfits

This third category corresponds, very largely, to that which is comprised in Dr. Hacker's category of "crazies." These are the truly mentally disturbed individuals who, for dark purposes of their own and subject to their own scheme of reality, have decided to embark upon some terroristic enterprise. These people may not be sufficiently abnormal to make their behavior the subject of attention by law enforcement authorities or others, and they may be quite masterful at disguising their abnormalities. They may not, necessarily, be suffering from any diagnosed mental illness. Nevertheless, they are, on analysis, a distinctly abnormal group; and their particular mental disturbance promotes. Such person embark on a wide variety of activity which is of a terror-producing character; and what marks them out from the true terrorist, particularly those who are politically organized, is the lack of purpose in the utilization of the terror generated. Terror is usually an incidental by-product of their distorted ideation. The objective of the terroristic misfit is very often revenge or some form of personal or social redress, and they are sometimes persons who have borne a grudge or have been traumatized by events in some way that they feel necessary to respond to by recourse to this form of violence. They have a singular fixation about the way they have been treated and may harbor a strong sense of grievance at an injustice, real or imaginary, done to them. Many of the lone bombers and fire setters would fall into this category. They are often lonely, unsuccessful, inadequate persons having a keen sense of personal failure for which they can only compensate or atone by some violent, dramatic act. A large number of the skyjackers, both domestic and international, are also conveniently classified in this way.

Such persons range from the near normal, psychopathic individual to the plainly psychotic. Resort to terrorism is not a symptom of any particular type of mental illness. The range of mental disturbance comprised in this class is virtually limitless and defies useful classification. Once again, the most useful taxonomy is developed from an examination of the activities, in the first place, rather than the actors themselves. While, for example, individuals of this category might engage in hostage taking, very often under extremely bizarre circumstances, they do not usually engage in kidnapping, which is a crime requiring much preparation and a certain amount of thought for future developments. Their acts tend to be somewhat spontaneous and responsive to the stimulus of the moment rather than the product of long and careful preparation. Many are overcontrolled types whose sudden, long repressed exposure is simply the sudden overt manifestation of a long-hidden inner process.[38] Some inadequate personalities, however, are very often given to lengthy periods of preparation in which the terroristic act if thought over and developed, usually without too much specificity[39] Some precipitating act, or the presentation of an unexpected opportunity, will often galvanize them into action. The act itself, when it occurs, is often the product of a hasty translation of this period of gestation into action and, for that reason alone it is often a failure. The behavior of Arthur Bremer, who attempted the assassination of Governor George Wallace, is instructive in this regard.[40]

The propensity of such types for causing harm is very considerable, and their emergence for the purposes of committing some act of this sort is often quite surprising because there may be no previous law enforcement intelligence about them. Their activities are much less predictable than those of other groups. The response to them must almost always be reactive. They are particularly prone to undertake bombings, especially those that do not require a great deal of sophistication or technical knowledge, and also assassination with the use of firearms. Many of the assassins of United States Presidents would fit the category described as "terroristic misfits."[41] A majority of the anarchist terrorists around the turn of the century would fit such a description. It is usually very easy to see, after the fact, that these individuals had such tendencies and had evidenced, by their behavior, those tendencies that suggested a propensity for harm directed against some individual. A surprising number of such persons pass security screening and find employment in sensitive positions that encourage them in or facilitate their designs. This is often due to a lack of proper psychological testing and is a serious security weakness. It is very easy to discount some of these individuals as being harmless, notwithstanding the specific character of the threats that they utter, and it is always a matter of surprise that they have acted as they stated they would. The potentiality of these misfits for harming the persons they threaten should never be minimized and, where information is received by way of direct communication of threats or otherwise, suggestive of harmful activity by such persons, the information should be taken very seriously indeed.[42] Many of these person are very persistent and will wait for an opportunity to act despite earlier action taken to discourage them.

NOTES

1. Yonah Alexander and Seymour Maxwell Finger, eds., "The Politics of Atrocity," *Terrorism: Interdisciplinary Perspectives* (New York: John Jay Press, 1977), p. 46.
2. There is really no such thing as *a* terrorist. Those who engage in the types of activity that would be characterized as terrorism are so varied in every respect that it is pointless trying to produce anything in the nature of a brief composite description of them.
3. *Disorders and Terrorism* (Washington, D.C.: U.S. Government Printing Office, 1977), p. 5.
4. New York: W.W. Norton, 1976.
5. It must be noted that names, as such, are neither revealing nor particularly helpful by way of identification. Nomen-

clature changes, as do affiliations. Many transformations take place even in groups with a strong ideological or nationalistic base. For interesting examples of the processes at work, see Thomas Kiernan, *Arafat* (New York: W.W. Norton, 1976). An interesting, but somewhat outdated, list and description is contained in *Transnational Terrorism* by Brian Crozier (Gaithersburg, Md.: International Association of Chiefs of Police, 1974). For a current update, see *Annual of Power and Conflict, 1976-77* (London: Institute for the Study of Conflict).

6. The Red Brigades, a loose, ultra-left extremist organization responsible for much of Italy's current terrorist wave, has drawn heavily upon th experience and even personnel of Italy's criminal classes. It is distinguished, however, from these, as they are organized, by its own political objectives and its use of these tactics to wage warfare against the established government rather than for the purposes of private enrichment.

7. Ernesto "Che" Guevera is a popular figure in this regard and many groups sympathetic to the West German terrorists now bear his names. It is always useful to ask the question: Why was this name thought to be useful or important to the persons selecting it?

8. On the SLA, generally, see Vin McLellan and Paul Avery, *The Voices of Guns* (New York: G.P. Putnam's Sons, 1977).

9. See Yonah Alexander, "From Terrorism to War: The Anatomy of the Birth of Israel,"*International Terrorism* (New York: Ams Press, 1976), pp. 211-257.

10. See J. Bowyer Bell, "Strategy, Tactics, and Terror: An Irish Perspective," *International Terrorism* (New York: Ams Press, 1976), pp. 65-89.

11. On this, generally, see Jordan J. Paust, "Terrorism and the International Law of War," 64 *Military Law Review,* 1974, pp. 1-36.

12. See *Terrorism From Robespierre to Arafat,* pp. 449-468.

13. Christopher Dobson and Ronald Payne, *The Carlos Complex* (New York: G.P. Putnam's Sons, 1977).

14. See, for example, Walter W. Howard, "The Terrorists: How They Operate A Worldwide Network," *The Washington Post,* January 18, 1976.

15. *The Carlos Complex,* pp. 141-185.

16. On this, generally, see H.H.A. Cooper, *The Terrorist and*

His Victim, Hearing Before the Subcommittee on Criminal Laws and Procedures of the Committee on the Judiciary of the United States Senate (Wash., D.C.: U.S. Gov't Printing Office, 1977).

17. The PFLP leadership, for example, always directed its operations from "safe" countries such as Lebanon, Syria or South Yemen.

18. On March 1, 1973, Black September seized a number of hostages, including the American Ambassador Cleo A. Noel and other diplomats, in the Saudi Arabian Embassy in Khartoum. The action, resulting in the brutal deaths of three diplomats, was wholly directed, mainly in code, from outside the country; and on its conclusion the perpetrators surrendered to the authorities.

19. This is the really distinctive feature of the Hanafi Muslim operation in Washington, D.C. in March 1977. The leader in the seizure of the three buildings not only took part in the assault on one of them, but was contained therein throughout until his inevitable surrender.

20. See, for example, the interesting Top Security Research Project No. 2, "The Female Terrorist and Her Impact on Policing," *Top Security,* August, September, October, November, 1976. For a view of the Italian woman terrorist, see *Panorama,* December 13, 1977, pp. 55-57. On the West German women terrorists, see "Frauen im Untergrund: Etwas Irrationales," 33 *Der Spiegel,* 1977, p. 22

21. The evolution of the SLA is a good example of this. See, among the extensive literature on the subject, John Bryan, *This Soldier Still at War* (New York: Harcourt Brace Jovanovich, 1975).

22. This has been the case, particularly, with the Fedayeen, the Palestinian terrorists whose very name means "sacrificers." The operations undertaken in Israel have been of a truly suicidal character, and those undertaking them were low level operatives left in no doubt about the slim prospects for survival.

23. It has been most pertinently said in another context: "Those who've given up crime now and reformed, they're no good, they're dead butterflies, their mental processes have atrophied—they've got too far away from it, mentally, I mean." Tony Parker and Robert Allerton, *The Courage of His Convictions* (New York: W.W. Norton, 1962), p. 108.

24. Compare, for example, the photographs of "Carlos" in Colin Smith, *Carlos: Portrait of a Terrorist* (New York: Holt Rinehart Winston, 1976) and that in the CIA Research Study, *International and Transnational Terrorism: Diagnosis and Prognosis,* PR76 10030, April 1976.
25. See H.H.A. Cooper, "What Is A Terrorist? A Psychological Perspective," 1 *Legal Medical Quarterly,* no. 1, March 1977, pp. 16-32.
26. This has been evidenced in a number of comparatively recent cases, including those of the train hijacking at Beilen, Entebbe, Mogadishu, and the Hanafi incident in Washington, D.C.
27. See Peter Clyne, *An Anatomy of a Skyjacking* (London: Abelard-Schuman, 1973).
28. *Disorders and Terrorism,* p. 5.
29. An extensive bibliography is available on Mafia and other organized crime terror. See, for example, Nicholas Gage, *Mafia, U.S.A.* (Chicago, Ill.: Playboy Press, 1962). A number of features of organized crime terror are worthy of close study and comparison with the tactics and techniques of political terrorists. It rarely involves "innocents," that is, persons having no dealings with organized crime. It is tightly controlled. Victims are not killed in certain "protected" places or in front of their families. Compare, in this latter regard, the killings undertaken by terrorists in Northern Ireland.
30. The notable successes, though using different methods, of the New York City Police Department and the Los Angeles Police Department, are well-known in law enforcement circles; and this experience has been widely shared through seminars and training sessions throughout the country. The FBI, through its academy at Quantico, has provided much useful instruction, as have its traveling teams. The IACP training programs have refined and disseminated this collective experience to a wide range of agencies, large and small.
31. The hostage-taker is a problem-causer, not a problem solver. He rarely thinks his operation through to its logical end. In consequence, he locks himself into a situation from which he has to be extricated as painlessly as possible by those competent to do his thinking for him.
32. On this, see Passim, *The Skyjacker.*

33. This is borne out by a number of tragic outcomes of sky-jackings during 1977-78 inspired by the necessary violence used by the West Germans at Mogadishu. A near disaster in Paris, two skyjackers with injuries in Pakistan, and a suicide in Atlanta should convince those responsible for the response that there are important distinctions to be understood and observed if tragedy is to be avoided.

34. The motivation was clearly personal rather than political, and, despite the military-style operation, organization and planning were poor. The whole matter, in retrospect, is to be seen as little more than an acting out of the hurt and frustration of the principal protagonist.

35 Idries Shah, "When rats are trapped they will try and will believe anything," *Reflections* (Penguin Books, 1972), p. 30.

36. See "The Inadequate Psychopath: Some Medico-Legal Problems and a Clinical Profile," 21 *Chitty's Law Journal,* no. 10, December 1973, pp. 325-343.

37. On this, generally, see H.H.A. Cooper, "Penal Policy and the Dangerous Offender: Remember the Poor Baker," 22 *Chitty's Law Journal,* no. 6, 1974, p. 191.

38. As seems to have been the case with Anthony Kiritsis who, in February 1977, took a mortgage company manager hostage in Indianapolis amid a blaze of publicity, wiring a loaded shotgun to his neck. Kiritsis was found insane by a jury on October 21, 1977.

39. George Metesky, the so-called "Mad Bomber" who placed explosive devices throughout Manhattan during the 1950's in consequence of a grudge against Consolidated Edison, is a good example. Both his bombs and his techniques improved as his campaign developed.

40. For much instructive material see Arthur H. Bremer, *An Assassin's Diary* (New York: Harper's Magazine Press, 1973).

41. See *Assassination and Political Violence,* pp. 62-67.

42. The seriousness with which such threats are generally regarded by the United States Courts is reflected in the heavy sentences imposed on those convicted of uttering them. In November 1977, Sylvester Chatman was sentenced in Tucson, Arizona, to five years imprisonment for telling Secret Service agents that he might "kill Carter or the Governor or the Mayor."

Terrorism: When and Where

"Barring some unique transformation in the nature of man or his institutions, transnational terror and revolutionary violence will be with us in the future, just as they have been with us for centuries past. Even in relatively stable, democratic, developed societies, events of the last decade revealed schisms that have produced mobs, bombings, and even gunfire in the streets. Even advanced authoritarian regimes with the resources and will to repress ruthlessly any open dissent have not always been able to impose order."

J. Bowyer Bell[1]

No age can regard itself as immune from the horrors of terrorism. Terrorism has occurred during times of great political stress and upheaval as well as during more tranquil times. Nevertheless, terrorism is a curiously cyclical phenomenon occurring intensely at some times only to abate suddenly and be entirely absent at others. It will then, almost inexplicably, recur, even in the same place, or elsewhere, in the same form, or in a mutation of it. Sometimes the abatement, or breathing space, has a rational explanation; it is a type of armistice or truce. At others, external or internal forces will have weakened the terroristic impulse so as to bring about a cessation of this activity. There have been a number of recurrent episodes of terrorism, curiously similar in their manifestations and the personalities of those who have engendered them, within the last hundred years. The same mix or blend seems to give rise to very much the same end product. The Anarchists at the end of the last century were extremely active throughout Europe and in some parts of the United States.[2] While among them there existed wide variations of belief and aims, they were all characterized by a near-pathological hatred of government and the "system" and a somewhat naive belief that something better would surely come out of the chaos they hoped to create. They assassinated large numbers of heads of state and other dignitaries and, viewed from the perspective of the times, their actions seemed to be almost beyond control. With hindsight, their actions, though tragic for individuals, and in some cases for the fate of nations, had little of the effect they had anticipated. The hated "system" did not disappear, and other rulers rapidly replaced those struck down. The Anarchists of yesteryear lacked the means to generalize chaos or to profit from it, had they been able to produce it. The protagonists of those forms of terrorism and their methods and beliefs are strikingly similar to those who are currently engaged in much the same work in different parts of the world. The "new terrorists," seen from this standpoint, are not so very different from the old. Their activities can usually be related, in some way, to existing political, social, or economic conditions; and their activities and abatement can be seen, too, as a reflection of the responses of the community to them.

Some organized terrorist groups have an extremely long history. So, too, do the struggles in which they have been engaged. The IRA, for example, can trace its history back to the 18th century; and, certainly in the form in which its political objectives are stated today, it has a record of continuous activity of more than sixty years. This is quite a long life for any political movement. Over that time, however, there have been very definite changes in both philosophy and methods, and those who take part in some of the more extreme acts of violence perpetrated by that body today would have some difficulty in reconciling them with the aims and objectives of their forebears.[3] Unquestionably, even an organization so traditional and quasi-official as the IRA has been quite radically altered by the influences of the modern philosophies of violence and revolution that owe more to their foreign, anarchist, or immediate Marxist-Leninist forebears than to the pure, Nationalistic aims espoused by the founding members of the IRA. The Provisional Wing of the IRA is a classic example of this trend. Terrorism is, therefore, a constantly evolving phenomenon that reflects the thinking and fashions of the age as well as the resources and technological developments that can be put to the service of those who use these methods in the struggle against established authority.

There are usually some clear pointers to the likelihood of terroristic activity by an examination of the existing conditions in the area where such activity takes place. A clinical examination of the body politic usually reveals signs of this disease even before it starts to take its toll. This is particularly so in the case of those groups that have some specific territorial alignment. Terroristic movements of this sort rarely grow up overnight. They are responses to social and political stimuli that can be clearly observed. The existence of unstable, near revolutionary conditions, a deteriorating economy, massive unemployment, foreign domination or exploitation, deep racial, ethnic or religious divisions, and all the other indicia of social unrest, might be expected to produce the reactions that are characterized as terroristic. The fact that they do not, where they might reasonably have been expected to, is often a very interesting and rewarding subject of study. There are always a large number of areas in the world where these disturbed conditions exist, and the fact of the association of organized terrorist groups with these areas and their prospects of altering the conditions therein is little more than a matter of keeping detailed progress records. Those having business or professional interests in, say, Northern Ireland, Argentina, or Lebanon would be very foolish to ignore the history, level of activity, and probable future operations of known terrorist groups operating in these areas. At any particular time, the United States Department of State and the Department of

Commerce can usually advise businessmen and others on the state of affairs in any particular territory in which they might have an interest. Such information can be very valuable in preparing to meet the hazards likely to be encountered. Constant, expert debriefing of those who have been recently on the scene is important. Official bodies will keep careful intelligence records of their own and will generally be able to observe developing trends so as to predict, with a fair degree of accuracy, the likelihood of a terrorist outbreak attributable to organized, territorially aligned groups in any particular part of the world. The need for keeping this information under constant, expert review is stressed. Patterns of terrorism, often stable for long periods, are capable of rapid change. Sometimes even last week's information is too old to be relied upon safely.

The trends and direction of the terrorism of the non-territorially aligned groups are very much more difficult to predict. While many of the same factors will be relevant to the analysis, their relationship to each other and the precipitating element is less clear. These groups tend to be opportunistic and often lie dormant for long periods awaiting the moment to strike to the greatest advantage. The fact that they have not committed an act of violence or engaged in overt activity for some time does not necessarily mean that they are no longer operational or have been disbanded. Very often, successful counteraction against these groups leads to their shifting their geographic sphere of activity or regrouping and going still further underground. Security forces cannot afford to lose sight of such groups or of the individual members of them. Terrorism can be a very malignant and persistent disease. The fact that a group appears to have been satisfactorily eliminated from the scene at any particular moment does not necessarily mean that its activities have finally ceased or that the memory of it has been totally lost. Unlike territorially aligned groups that gain political legitimacy so that the very reason for their existence disappears, some of these other groups always have unfinished business. Many of the seemingly extinct groups re-emerge in some form or another, almost phoenix-like, as a result of a changed set of circumstances that seem to promise the prospects of future successful activity. The remnants of one group often attach themselves to another in the course of formation, as happened with the West German groups.[4] The new organism is often more virulent than the old. Even the most random outbreaks of terrorism generally have a discernible pattern about them when all the data is available. The ground must be ready before the seed can be sown.

Terrorists generally strike where they feel the enemy is weakest and least able to resist the forces that they are able to focus upon this area. Attacks by terrorists of this sort are rarely haphazard and are often carefully planned over a long period of time. While, to a large extent, the terrorist is able to choose the time and place of any individual action, he is generally as much a prisoner of events as anyone else. Any terroristic campaign takes a considerable amount of time to plan and develop, and, if it is to succeed in any way, the conditions must be right for it. Even the most nihilistic terrorism does not take place in a socio-political vacuum. The terrorist tends to take advantage of events rather than produce them by his own hand. Terroristic enterprises are rarely mounted out of the blue. What does occur is that the warning signs are not properly appreciated or are ignored. There are, thus, useful indicators of when terrorism is likely to occur even in the case of the non-territorially aligned, anarchistic groups. Considerable statistical work has been done by different agencies of the United States government, notably by the CIA,[5] but the data that have been collected is often imperfect and inadequately presented so as to be able to make a true predictive judgment. Inadequate arrangements for the exchange of information on an international basis have also hampered these efforts, a circumstance that greatly favored those groups operating in Europe.

Where terrorism is likely to occur is, again, a matter for careful analysis, taking into account the character of the groups involved, their strength, and their objectives. In contested territories, where basic political dispute has the character of a power struggle among different domestic groups, terrorism will usually be confined to a specific geographical area. Terrorism produced by the disturbed conditions in Lebanon, for example, has not generally extended beyond the borders of that country. The possiblity of the involvement of strangers to the struggle—other than on an accidental basis—even though they might be in the territory concerned, is to be determined by the degree of sophistication of the groups concerned, their appreciation of the utility of involving foreigners, and their political objectives. If the terrorists are manifestly hostile to foreigners—for example, if they are engaged in a struggle designed to bring into being a left-wing government, the declared aims of which are the exclusion of foreign capital and business—it may well be that persons associated with these interests will be the subject of deliberate attack in the course of the power struggle. Some foreigners will be higher risk targets than others. This has been the case, notably in many Latin American countries. Anti-imperialist, anti-capitalist, Marxist-Leninist, or Maoist groups can be expected to pick targets representative of United States interests. On the other hand, many of the groups are concerned only with their internal or domestic power structures and are anxious not to alienate foreign support. Foreigners would continue to lead relatively safe, if somewhat nerve-wracking, existences. In such countries, foreign victims would be incidental rather than a chosen target of terrorist groups. The possibilities of accidental victimization are high in such places, and the restrictions imposed by even minimal, common sense security can be costly in psychological and material terms. Areas where such strife is commonplace, such as Lebanon or Ethiopia, are best avoided by those who do not have essential business in those countries, regardless of their identification with particular interests that may make them evident terrorist targets. Such countries are likely to have a long-term terrorism problem; and security, in personal and corporate terms, has to be reckoned as a necessary cost of doing business in the area. Government, of course, cannot afford to be driven out; and it may be that other interests, too, would consider abandonment of their interests a matter that they could not afford, however great the terrorist pressure.

Many countries in Europe can now be identified as having a severe terrorist problem. Italy is a case in point.[6] The number of potential victims has grown considerably in the last few years. The range of target individuals has been greatly extended. Persons having interests in that country should carefully study the regional manifestations of terrorism and take advice from experts on the region as well, if possible, such as the local law enforcement authorities. Some urban areas in particular are more dangerous than others. Some terrorism is local in character, butt much is now related to wider, global movements. Much of this terrorism is of an endemic, long-standing character, but has lately been intensified as the economic problems of the country have grown worse. Politically, Italy is very unstable, having had nearly forty governments since the fall of Mussolini. The political struggle that has left the parties of the moderate and extreme left in a virtually polarized position, as well as the effects of the overall world power struggle, must also be taken into account in assessing the terrorist prospects. It must be remembered, too, that Italy is a manufacturing country having virtually no raw materials of her own. This leaves the country peculiarly at the mercy of world market trends, and the effects of these on the nation's economy are an important pointer to possible terrorist activity.

The ease and rapidity of modern communications have, undoubtedly, enlarged the terrorist problem. The problem of the West German terrorists has now spilled over into neighboring countries—particularly France, Holland, Switzerland and Austria—and these terrorists are operating out of those countries, not only against German targets but against foreigners who might be thought to be involved in frustrating their aims and objectives. While they suffered serious reverses during 1977, the threat they represent cannot be felt to be at an end. They have, in the past, attacked mainly West German targets, but there is no assurance that the pattern of operations will continue indefinitely. Their threats against the West German national airlines were very successful in influencing West Germans and foreigners alike to withdraw their business. The modern transnational terrorist is likely to operate anywhere and will choose the sphere of his operations by reference to the locality of the target rather than by reference to some other more specific geographic aim. The sphere of operations can change very rapidly, and information regarding it must be up-to-date to be of value for security purposes.

The best protective measure against terrorism is to avoid it. This is so in the strategic as well as the more immediate tactical sense. Those who frequent high-crime areas stand a greater chance of being victimized than those who do not. Where there is a scene of considerable terrorist activity, on whatever account, if that area can be avoided, the prospects of harm are naturally reduced. There is no philosophical point to be made here; tourists and sightseers should simply avoid battlefields while the war is raging. Foreigners should always avoid areas of contention and, particularly, riots and civil disturbances. Only essential personnel should be sent to or kept in an area of intense terroristic activity, and the best protective measures must be taken in the case of those who are, inevitably, so exposed. The first rule of this business is: *Know the real trouble spots.* Where areas of the world are clearly determined to be those in which a high degree of terroristic activity is taking place or can be reasonably expected in the near future, an assessment must be made as to the degree of risk imposed upon those who have to undertake the task of visiting them or living in them. Human, as well as purely economic factors, must always be taken into account. It may well be that certain persons or nationalities will be exposed to a greater risk than others by presenting themselves in those areas. Families, for example, may sometimes pose a greater security risk than individuals living in protected compounds and submitted to a strict regimen of security during both working and social hours. The objective in every case should be to reduce the magnitude of the risk by avoidance rather than having to meet a known threat by taking protective measures against it. This will often involve much system-wide planning and a certain amount of restriction on individual freedom of choice.

Modern transportation systems pose a very inviting target to terrorist groups. They are very exposed and difficult to protect without a great deal of inconvenience to those who use and operate them. Not only are terrorists able to disrupt an important social and commercial activity by attacking them, but they can, by this means, affect international relations in a significant way. A wide variety of nationalities can be found using each other's transportation systems quite indiscriminately. The most important and dramatic form of interference of this type with transportation is skyjacking. This, basically, is the seizure of control of an aircraft in flight. It can, obviously, occur in almost any part of the world's airways despite the legal measures that have been enacted to counteract it and the practical security steps that have been taken, on the ground and in the air, to frustrate terroristic endeavors.

The threat of skyjacking is not universally even; some areas and some airlines are more prone to be targets than others. Airport security, in particular, varies very widely from country to country, and even from region to region, and many international hijackings have been deliberately commenced in airports, such as those of Athens and Madrid where the screening precautions were not as stringent as elsewhere.[7] Some countries put considerations of security below the need to avoid inconveniencing travelers, with a view to promoting and maintaining tourism. Searches are perfunctory or not undertaken at all. These facts should be known and taken into account by those who are engaged in providing protective services. The itineraries of sensitive persons should take such facts into account. Wherever probable, airports with deficient security procedures should be avoided. Some airlines, particularly airlines having a national identification or affiliation, are also more sensitive targets in different places and at different times. The threats made in November 1977 against Lufthansa Airlines, in consequence of the reverses then suffered by the West German terrorists, are indicative of the potentialities for terrorist action against certain carriers and the way in which these threats can develop.[8] It would be foolish for those concerned with individual security to ignore such threats.

Skyjacking is a form of activity that is particularly prone to the contagion effect, and a spectacular skyjacking by a politically organized group is not infrequently followed by others that are carried out by those who have been designated quasi-terrorists or by terroristic misfits. These events are widely reported, in great detail, with much attention to the methods employed by the skyjackers. These activities, again, tend to follow a pattern that is important from the perspective of those who are planning the protective responses. Trends can usually be spotted and sometimes quite accurately predicted. Modifications of procedures and equipment can be undertaken to meet the anticipated threat. Some airlines that, in the past, have been the subject of very intense terrorist attack, such as the Israeli Airline, El Al, have so improved their security procedures and the safety of their equipment that they are, in some ways, safer to fly with than those that have been less frequent targets. Such security is costly, and it is rarely undertaken on a voluntary, precautionary basis. It must always be taken into account that the frustration produced by these measures in those terrorist groups who continue to desire to harm these airlines might result in even more bizarre attacks, such as bombings and the like, which could involve those even remotely associated with a particular airline's operations. Terrorist action taken on the ground, as a result of the inability to board an aircraft, is most likely to spill over into other areas and claim innocent victims.

From a security perspective, the *when* and the *where* of terrorism have also an even more personal, tactical application. The planning of individual security turns substantially on these factors. It must be carefully considered where and when an individual target figure is likely to be most vulnerable. The setting up of an effective system of protection depends to a large extent on how well these calculations are made. Broadly speaking, every individual will have a principal place of residence or some abode at which a substantial part of his leisure and restful hours will be spent; he will have a principal and, perhaps, subsidiary place or places of business at which the greater part of his working activities will take place. He will have to visit various places and will have to traverse the various routes that connect all those different places. He will be vulnerable to different types of attack, in different degrees, in each of those places; and each activity undertaken presents a distinctive security problem of its own. An attack upon a man's home may be quite a different propostion from an attack upon his place of business, and different again from what is involved in an attempt on his life while he is traveling between the two.

Certain measures can be taken to improve the security of a residence to the point that it becomes almost an impregnable fortress. Whether such measures are worthwhile depends upon the type of risk that it is prudently estimated the target figure faces in his own home. These measures are of little overall value, however, if the individual has to make relatively unprotected journeys from his residence to various other places with which his interests can be identified. His vulnerability on such journeys becomes a factor taken into account by terrorists in *their* planning of how and where an attack upon him might be made.

An overall, systematic approach to security is required to ensure that each of the points at which the individual is likely to present himself as a target are adequately covered to give him *the security that he needs.* Those needs may be very diverse, but they will always be related in a distinctive way to the individual, his location, and a particular point in time. Much data is necessary for any useful evaluation. A very careful risk assessment must be undertaken to determine *where* the individual is likely to be most vulnerable. This factor will often decide *how* an attack on his person is to be made and what form it will take. If it is determined that he is likely to be especially vulnerable while in his home, then special security measures may need to be instituted to reduce the vulnerability factor in that area. As a first requisite, entry must be restricted and controlled, and this should be done with a minimum of inconvenience to those who live and work in that place. Communications need to be improved. Background checks will need to be conducted on servants and others having frequent access to the premises. Some structural alteration may need to be undertaken. The full weight of the protective effort should never, however, be expended on reducing the vulnerability of a single area, as this only invites terroristic attention elsewhere. If it is too difficult to attack the target figure in his own residence, other possibilities will need to be considered. A comprehensive security assessment effort is needed to provide protection where, from a careful study of the matter, it is determined to be needed most. While an individual's overall security may need improvement, some areas will usually need more attention than others.

The *where* and the *when* of terrorism, in this latter, more personal sense, will also determine the nature and quality of the protection that is to be offered. These factors will often determine what, practically, *can* be offered. The *where* and *when* in the wider sense may also be a material consideration; some countries, for example, do not allow the use of armed bodyguards. The type of protection that might be necessary to reduce the vulnerability of the target figure in his residence may well be of little or no value when he is in the course of being transported elsewhere. The type of protection that could well serve him in a public place might be odious and unnecessary in a private dwelling house. The only general protection an individual can enjoy is to be elsewhere when a terrorist attack occurs. This is only possible when it is *known* when and where such an attack is to take place. If this is known, *how* it is to take place is immaterial as far as the individual is concerned. A careful, overall survey of security needs must be taken in relation to where and when the target figure is likely to present himself as a serious or possible object of terrorist attack. Nothing should be overlooked. Kidnapping is often easiest when the prospective victim is on the move, but kidnappings have taken place from the victims' residences and places of business. For effective security planning, all contingencies should be provided for, and the whereabouts of the protected individual and those through whom he might be put at risk at any particular point in time is of the utmost importance. *The objective, always, should be to avoid placing the target figure in a position where he is likely to be exposed to harm.* Once again, it will be seen that there is no real substitute for hard information. The better the data, the more effective the protection.

NOTES

1. *Transnational Terror,* (Washington, D.C.: AEI-Hoover Policy Studies, 1975), p. 69.
2. For a good, broad overview see Barbara Tuchman, *The Proud Tower* (New York: Bantam Books, 1972), pp. 72-132.
3. A distinguished Irish jurist, Sean MacBride, a one-time member of the IRA and now United Nations Commissioner for Namibia, has said: "The things which are done today by what you call terrorist movements—take the IRA—would not have been dreamt of in the IRA I knew 20 or 30 years ago." *Skeptic,* Issue No. 11, January/February, 1976. p. 11.
4. See, generally, "Stark genug, den Kriegzuerklaren? 38 *Der Spiegel,* 1977, p. 17.
5. Particularly through the ITERATE project. See Edward F. Mickolus in *Terrorism: Interdisciplinary Perspective,* Yonah Alexander and Seymour Maxwell Finger, eds., (New York: John Jay Press, 1977), pp. 209-269.
6. Italy had over 2,000 political bombings during 1977. Kidnappings have steadily escalated with 62 in 1975 to 76 in 1977. There are over a hundred known extremist political organizations currently active. Law enforcement efforts have been notably hampered by the country's unstable political and economic situation and an ineffective system of criminal process.
7. This is what lies behind the provisions of S2236, a bill before the United States Senate in 1977-78, entitled "List of Dangerous Foreign Airports." The bill provisions would have an admonitory character, but sanctions are also proposed.
8. The threats serve the terrorist purpose even though they do not materialize, for protective measures, costly in themselves, must be increased wherever the airline operates. Losses on passenger traffic and freight can be substantial as Lufthansa found.

Reducing the Risk

"Trust in God—but tie your camel first."
Sayings of the Prophet

Having identified the nature of the threat, who is likely to pose it, something of the methods and techniques that might be used, the probable targets, and the time and place that it might materialize, those concerned with the provision of protective services must address themselves to the means for minimizing the harm likely to be caused. *The keynote of these recommendations is preparation and planning.*[1] The preparation and planning undertaken by terrorists in order to be able to carry out their tasks must be matched by those who are providing protection and necessary countermeasures. Hastily prepared defenses are generally extremely costly and rarely effective. The risks are rarely perceived in the right proportions or perspective and haste often produces overreaction. Careful preparation and planning demand forethought, training, and the assembly of a variety of skills and materials for the task in hand. This is not a task that can be entered into lightly or undertaken other than in a methodical, professional fashion. Handling the problems posed by terrorists is not a job for the "do-it-yourselfer." *Terrorism is serious business.* The protagonists of terrorism should never be underrated. They start with many advantages. Certain natural factors favor their enterprises, and the task of those who are providing personal and organizational security is made more difficult by this unfavorable balance of advantages. Those providing protective services must address themselves to the problem of evening up the score. Careful *planning* and *preparation* help to reduce the advantages that the terrorist is given by virtue of his ability to use surprise and initiative in mounting his own operations.

Contingency planning is, therefore, of the highest importance. This must be of a comprehensive nature and should seek to integrate all aspects of the protective system in a way that is feasible and cost-effective. It should be remembered that any alteration of the planned response so as to produce an altered response in one sector will cause an alteration or imbalance in another. If time, money, and energy are put into a certain area of protective services a certain return can be expected. That anticipated return will alter if the expenditures are changed in any way. The real difficulty lies in measuring the return in relation to what is expended. What gives greater security (as distinct from a *feeling* of security), more bodyguards or an electronic alarm system? An appropriate balance must be struck between hard and soft responses. The contingency plan must be sufficiently flexible to meet changing situations and to accommodate growth and expansion. Above all, a contingency plan must be constantly updated as new information and altered circumstances are fed into it. Those who are affected by these planning arrangements must be made aware of the alterations and the changing expectations produced by them. The provision of protective services is an ongoing business. The responsibilities of those engaged in providing them never cease. Terrorism is aided and abetted when the system grows sluggish, backward-looking, and fails to grow with events.

Planning and preparation must commence with an expert survey of security needs. If this cannot be done in-house, then the task must be entrusted to a responsible, independent expert. While the resident security expert will often have the advantage of familiarity with the organizations personnel and procedures, he may lack specialized knowledge in the area of terrorism.[2] As in all matters, care must be taken to ensure that the advice sought is delivered by properly qualified persons having the skills and experience commensurate with the task set for them. That task must be identified in general terms before expert assistance can be engaged. If the security needs are of an unusual kind or demand special skills or experience, it may be necessary for this to be brought in from outside, whether or not there is an in-house security specialist or department. Time and money expended at this stage will be recouped later. Once the overall security needs have been evaluated, a concise report should be drawn up for the consideration of a small *security oversight committee.* This committee should be responsible for making security recommendations to the chief executive of the organization concerned, and those recommendations, when accepted, should be put into effect by a permanent department established for the purpose. The committee, comprised of non-security specialists, should bring together the widest variety of skills and a thorough familiarity with the overall needs, personnel and resources of the organization. The oversight committee should have general supervisory functions in relation to the implementation of recommendations and should meet periodically to review the way in which the security system is working. It is stressed here that the oversight committee should take real responsibility in those matters and not regard itself as a pro-forma body. Overall day-to-day management of security matters should, however, be entrusted to the appropriate permanent department. Such a system gives a proper blend of lay and technical participation.

162

To a certain extent, preparation is a speculative exercise. Preparation to meet the terrorist involves, in part, being able to think along the same lines as those of a potential terrorist. This is not easy for those who have been constantly engaged in lawful pursuits and, in particular, in the combatting of antisocial forces. There is a kind of rigidity and a certain puritanical approach which tends to inhibit the practitioners of public or private law enforcement from truly thinking along terroristic lines. Nevertheless, it is a useful, practical exercise to utilize one's professional skills to try to determine how the enterprise being protected might be attacked by those wishing to do it irreparable harm. Such systematic speculation is an essential part of preparation and planning. The system should be constantly checked and tested by those responsible for its security in order to see whether the defenses they have erected against surprise attack are effective for the purpose. Proper supervision and inspection of the system are an essential part of its efficient functioning. All security systems have a human element, a procedural element, and a material element. Each of these requires constant, separate testing in order to find out its weaknesses. Systems rarely have a uniform strength. On many occasions, the procedural element, while theoretically effective, will be found to be deficient as a result of human error. On the other hand, if security equipment is not properly used or is ineffectively located, it will be of no value, however effective might be the performance of the human beings entrusted with its use. Care must be taken that these factors do not cancel each other out. For this reason, it is essential that the system be tested as an integrated whole by someone having a panoramic view of what is required of it. Wherever possible, security systems should be uncomplicated. The more complicated the system is, the more likely it is to produce human error that will cause it to fail at a crucial moment.

Equipment should be appropriate, sound, and well-functioning; the human agents should be prepared in its use and given constant training and supervision in whatever is required of them. Well-trained personnel react smoothly and efficiently in an emergency. The nature of the training is of the highest importance. Personnel act in a way in which they have been trained. If their training has encouraged rigid adherence to the rules, they will not be sufficiently flexible to meet the type of emergency that clever terrorists are likely to produce. Training must be designed to produce a thoughtful response, one capable of modification as circumstances demand. Well-trained personnel know not only *what* to do but *why* they are doing it. The initiative of the terrorist must be met with equal initiative and ingenuity on the part of those who are responding. Security services should be kept in a constant state of preparedness. They must be periodically tested with "mock" exercises and maintained at the proper pitch. If security personnel are not alert and ready to move when an emergency occurs the delay may well be fatal. The worst thing that can occur for those engaged in the provision of protective services is to be lulled into a false sense of security. Disaster strikes when the guard is down.

Those engaged in the provision of protective services should make themselves acquainted with the value of the appropriate expert assistance. Many disciplines have much to offer in the fight against terrorism if their contributions are appropriately used. It is important to know, for example, what contribution a psychiatrist or psychologist might make and not to seek of them advice that is not within their domain.[3] Security experts must acquaint themselves with the contributions that other disciplines can make and know where they can call upon this expert assistance in an emergency. It is important to be familiar not only with the services that specialists can provide but also with how they might be reached in an hurry. Part of every contingency plan should be a roster of experts who might be rapidly called into action should the occasion present itself. Expert advice is no substitute for effective decision-making. But good decisions depend upon the advice sought, received and taken.

Communications are of the highest importance. If those responding in the event of a terrorist attack are unable to issue the appropriate directions to those under their command, or are unable to communicate effectively with those with whom they must collaborate, the counteroperation becomes extremely confused and chaotic. Organized terrorists often make communications systems a first point of attack. Reliable emergency communications systems should be set up and everybody concerned with them in any way should be aware of how they operate and with whom they can communicate by those means. There should always be a clear chain of command so that, in an emergency, everyone is aware of the place to which he must go, the way in which he must respond, and from whom he ought to take orders. Communications systems must be simple and secure and proof against being used to disseminate false orders and information. The contingency plan should show very clearly the way in which the communications will operate under unusual conditions and the way in which emergency communications and directives will be issued and handled. *It should be presumed that in any serious terroristic enterprise there will be an attempt to interfere with communications.* This may be done to produce disorganization in the course of some violent operation, or there may be electronic surveillance conducted in order to gather information about the organization, individual or institution to be attacked. Good security involves keeping lines of communication free from interference at all times and ensuring that sensitive communications are not passed, whether in writing or by electronic means, to those who might make antisocial or other improper use of them.

Terrorists are always looking for information that will asist them in their undertakings. Very often careless utterances in public or even in what seem to be private communications fall into the hands of those who would make use of them for terroristic purposes or who whould be in a position to pass on these communications to those who would. *Careless talk costs lives.*[4] Those operating in foreign countries tend to be particularly prone to careless utterances, often assuming, quite wrongly, that the language they are speaking is not understood. In highly dangerous situations, the necessity for keeping confidences is generally well-appreciated. In seemingly less dangerous circumstances, security in this respect is rarely good. Many people simply do not realize the value of the information they impart in casual conversation. It should be remembered that terrorists are anxious to build up reliable dossiers of information regarding prospective targets. They will use any available means to get that information, including wiretapping, bribery and infiltration. Information regarding personalities, property, itineraries, habits, and other matters that would aid in planning a terroristic operation must be denied them. Personal information about corporate figures, particularly, should never be passed out to strangers by telephone, and biographical material utilized for publicity purposes should be carefully screened to see that it does not contain information of a sensitive nature. Documents containing information that might be of value to those planning some terroristic enterprise should be carefully safeguarded at all times and a proper transmission sequence and security classification process should be established. These procedures should be regularly reviewed by the security oversight committee.

A full biographical dossier with the most minute, intimate and personal details should be compiled by those responsible for security for every likely target figure. It goes without saying, in light of previous observations, that this material should be very carefully guarded indeed. It should be seen and handled by as few persons as possible. It is appreciated that many of those likely to be terrorist targets would resent this process as an intrusion upon their privacy, and it is often an exceedingly difficult "selling job" to get such persons to accept the need for this type of information to be kept at all. Much of the information can only be provided by them personally. It is essential, however, for the personal safety of such individuals that this information be readily available to those who would be able to assist in saving them from harm or rescuing them in the event that they fall into terrorist hands. Time is often of the essence in these situations. If time has to be spent on obtaining this information once the terroists have acted, it might well have fatal consequences for the victim. The type of information collected and stored will obviously vary from individual to individual, but it must always be sufficiently complete to provide an instant point of reference on almost every contingency that can be envisaged.

A crisis cannot be effectively managed by a committee. Information can be obtained by many agents, and certain work can be delegated to others; but many decisions will need to be made in the eventuality of certain terrorist actions that require a cool head and a decisive executive capacity. Consultation may well be necessary, but collective decison-making is a slow process. It is well a for definite crisis manager to be appointed in advance and for his responsibilities and powers to be clearly established. The principle applies equally to public as well as private agencies that have to cope with crises of this kind. It is sometimes necessary for such an individual, in the course of a crisis, to make decisions which might constitute an inconvenient or awkward precedent if translated to a later time. For this reason, consideration might be given to the appointment of a crisis manager on an expendable basis, so that once his useful functions have been served in the management of one incident he can be retired without prejudice from that postition and another appointed to take his place. His experience need not be lost, and he can be available for consultation by his successors. In the case of kidnapping or hostage taking, it is particularly necessary to provide a satisfactory outside support system for the victim who is, at the time, largely in a position of helplessness.[5] In the private sector, the individual managing the crisis is able to marshal the full resources of the organization at his disposal and coordinate his endeavors with the public authorities in the best interest of the victim. Cool, decisive action is called for; and this requires the assignment of a considerable amount of responsibility and authority in anticipation of such an event. The crisis manager should not be the head of the organization; but he must be able, on his own, to command all the resources he might need.

The accent should always be on preventive or precautionary measures. It is better to stop something unpleasant from happening than to have to cope with its consequences once it has occurred. Wherever security can be improved by the introduction of a new process or an improvement in personnel or procedures or the use of newer, more sophisticated equipment, this should be done. *It is better to be sure than sorry.* Terrorists quickly learn to adapt themselves to changing conditions. Even quite sophisticated technology becomes outdated. Constant updating improves morale. Where the improvements in security involve, for example, the use of new locks and new safety equipment, the cost of such precautionary measures is usually more than outweighed by the psychological feeling of security that it gives to those in whose behalf these measures have been taken. Care must be taken, however, not to develop a "siege mentality." Security should not ordinarily become obtrusive or of overwhelming concern. The constant preoccupation with security by those whose work is of a totally different order is often harmful to the nature of what they must do and can be a very stressful experience that can lower their performance and general enjoyment of life. Potential target figures must be relieved of as much of this stress as possible. For this reason, provision of security should be assigned to the appropriate experts on the view that it is *their* task to look after their charges rather than that those who are exposed to these abnormal risks should have to bear the additional burden of looking after themselves. The measures taken should be reassuring to the person being protected.

There are, nevertheless, those whose work, position, or location are likely to bring upon them additional risks that they will need to meet and cope with from their own resources. Comparatively few persons can have the luxury of a permanent body-guard, and it will be comparatively few persons in any organization that can have the benefit of constant surveillance and the skilled asistance and protection of a large, well-prepared security organization. Most persons will have to fend for themselves, and the degree of risk to which they are exposed will determine the amount of training and preparation *they* will need to meet it. In some cases, this will involve little more than their being apprised of the likely risks and being taught how to minimize their effects by relatively simple alterations of their ordinary patterns of behavior. In other cases, it will involve special training such as a course in defensive driving and, perhaps, the making of routine security checks or, in extreme cases, the handling of weapons. A careful, professional estimation must be made to determine what measure of training and what type is appropriate in each case. Training is expensive and, if given indiscriminately, can be counterproductive. In general, weapons training should only be given to those persons who are not merely competent in their use and fairly confident in their handling of them but who would have the temperament necessary to be able to use them in an emergency.[6] Weapons, especially handguns, can sometimes be dangerous placebos. Greater risks are often incurred by teaching unsuitable people to use weapons, or leaving them in charge of weapons that they are unable to use, than by denying them the possession of such armaments. Individuals living or working in isolated locations who have to travel long distances to reach a protected situation have a special responsibility for their own safety. Their prospective danger should never be increased by assigning them specially valuable property or sensitive information likely to attract attackers. Their needs and training should form part of the overall, integrated security pattern established for the organization, but their own responsiblities should be impressed upon them and they should be given every encouragement to meet these requirements. Adequate communications are very important in such cases, especially where these potential targets are on the move.

Fighting terrorism is, in the main, a team action. It requires organization and trust. There is no place here for the lone hero or for secretive, individual dealings with terrorist groups. Not only does this breed suspicion and cause difficulties within an organization, but it is rarely effective. The terrorist usually has a definite objective and has his own organization to meet the needs generated by the struggle to attain it. The individual seeking to pit himself against such an organization is at an obvious disadvantage. In seeking to outwit the terrorist he will often only succeed in outwitting those trying to protect him. High risk targets, if they are not constantly protected by an individual, personal bodyguard, should keep someone concerned with their security informed of their movements at all times. If possible, they should be in voice communication with someone in a security department at regular hours, and there should be prearranged code words or signals that will indicate that they are safe or otherwise. Such procedures should be kept relatively simple and foolproof, as far as possible, from the problems of false alarms. In the event of a serious security problem arising, those responsible for protective services need to have the greatest lead time possible so as to put their contingency plans into effect. For this reason, anything that can alert them to any mischance at an early stage might mean the difference between life or death for the potential victim.[7] The person protected should feel himself to be part of the team concerned with *his* safety.

The total security effort should encompass not only the presumed target figures themselves, but their familes and those through whom it might be expected that terrorists might strike. The terrorist seeks to coerce. Anyone or anything affording the opportunity for coercion must be considered a risk. The families must not only be given special instruction as to how to act in the event of anything happening to the principal target figure, but such instruction must also take into account their own responsiblities as a result of their relationship with that figure. These are not pleasant facts on which to dwell. Once more, this type of awareness should be inculcated without creating such a feeling of fear as is liable to jeopardize the work performance and living relationships of the individuals concerned. The creation of an atmosphere of high anxiety or tension can be so counterproductive as to produce disfunctions or even the retirement of the target figure from his assigned role. This, of course, is a way in which terrorists indirectly achieve their objectives. Family relationships are often a weak link at which the terrorist strikes. Many would risk themselves but would hesitate before exposing their families to danger. The impression must be given to families and others that the highest degree of security *is* being provided and that they have a very important role in cooperating with those who are undertaking the task of providing the protection. Family life styles may need to be sensibly re-designed so as to minimize risk.

The importance of avoiding terrorist situations or situations which have the potential for developing harm to a target figure cannot be over-stressed. Those who go looking for trouble generally find it. The terrorist's job is made easier by the risky behavior in which many individuals engage. The injunction not to engage in such behavior is especially needful for those working overseas. Certain areas or locations may be dangerous for foreigners. They should be avoided. Behavior that is antagonistic, antipathetic or politically imprudent should always be avoided in foreign countries. Foreigners should avoid drawing unpleasant attention to themselves. Quarrels with neighbors and other unseemly behavior are not merely prone to create problems of a civil nature but are also likely to be exploited by those anxious to hurt the individual concerned and the interests he represents. Travel time between home and place of work should be cut to the minimum. Corporations operating overseas in potentially difficult areas should consider having a "safe housing" policy where employees are grouped together in areas where they can be physically protected and offer each other mutual support. This is particularly necessary where government employees are concerned, and most government agencies are well used to the need for living in secure compounds in potentially sensitive areas. What cannot be avoided must be endured. While the effect of this on the quality of life is obvious, the ability of the individual to adapt, provided that he understands the necessity for this type of precaution, will enable him to overcome any of the unnatural stresses and strains that the situation would otherwise produce. Particular caution should be taken when on unfamiliar territory. Those who travel a great deal have a particular need to inform themselves about what they are likely to encounter. It is well to be prepared in every way by studying local customs and the current local situation. Until, however, a proper period of acclimatization has passed, the individual exposed to a new culture with which he is unfamiliar should take particular care about personal security, for he may well expose himself to risk he is unable to detect on account of his inability to understand incipient signs.

The introduction of new security procedures and the provision of sophisticated security equipment is a job for the expert. There should be no "do-it-yourself" security efforts, particularly in high risk areas. Not only does *this* type of personal protection run counter to the advice that has already been given regarding the provision of an integrated security system, but such lone efforts are usually quite ineffective and only serve to generate their own security problems. The properly equipped expert will have the data available to make a quick and effective appraisal, and he can take account of what is needed by reference to local conditions. Such expert advice should be meticulously followed. There is no point in trying to outguess or outsmart the expert. If there is no confidence in the expert chosen he should not have been employed in the first place. There are many pitfalls in providing personal security. Alarm systems, for example, can be extremely elaborate and expensive, but if they are not properly adjusted to the requirements of individual and group needs they are an unwarranted expense that can cause confusion and may serve to produce a hazard in times of need. Uniformity, especially in the matter of communications, is an important consideration. The most expensive device is not always the best or the one most suited for the matter in hand. What to use, and for what purpose, is often a matter of baffling fascination for the layman. There is, in particular, a proliferation of security equipment of all kinds on the market, and this is being constantly altered and updated. Only a reliable expert can tell what is suitable for the job in hand and what is likely to be excessive, over-luxurious, or even dangerous. *Generally speaking, the simpler the system, the less likely it is to cause confusion.*[8] This simplicity is, however, usually purchased at the cost of some effectiveness from the perspective of overall security. Once more, this is a matter for overall planning.

Keeping a low profile is an important part of overall risk reduction. In activities that require extensive publicity, such as politics and entertainment, this advice is, of course, contrary to the general policy that is likely to be pursued. The risks that are incurred by following such a policy must be fully appreciated and allowed for in any security system. Those who elect for a high profile or have this forced on them need special protection to match it. Keeping a low profile is very necessary in a hostile, alien environment and can contribute greatly to the safety of individuals who are seeking to avoid troublesome situations. When a situation of danger presents itself, such as a hostage taking, a skyjacking or kidnapping, the injunction to keep a low profile is doubly important. *The individual who draws attention to himself in such a situation is increasing his own jeopardy.* This has been tragically demonstrated on scores of occasions. Terrorists are generally prone to single out persons who have drawn attention to themselves by loud talk, threatening gestures or a posture of authority. Such behavior, although it may be natural to the individual concerned, is highly dangerous in the circumstances. A person who can appear to melt away into the background, or who can remain unobtrusive in a situation of danger so as to be lost among the crowd, stands a greater prospect of survival. All over-reactions should be avoided where possible, and a posture of calm watchfulness should be adopted. This is particularly necessary for those having an identifiable, official position. The watchword in all situations should be: *Keep calm.* The person who is observant and able to wait for his opportunity will often survive, whereas the individual who is prone to overdramatization and excessive reactions is usually unable to act in his own interests appropriately when the time comes. Again, training and advice in these matters can be helpful in cultivating the right attitude.

Forewarned is forearmed. The importance of maintaining an effective information system is so great that repetition on this account is excusable. *Nothing can be done in the area of counter-terrorism without the effective intelligence needed.* Informed decisions simply cannot be made unless the necessary data is available to the decision-makers. Within the limits allowed by law, the fullest possible information systems should be developed by government agencies, and by private organizations and individuals as appropriate to their needs. Storage of information is less important than knowing where to go for information when the need arises. Information exchange on a need-to-know basis should be arranged among those organizations that have a compatible identity of interests, and constant passage of information between the public and private sectors will ensure that the best possible quality of intelligence is available to those who have to make the decisions. The gathering of information is particularly important because information can, obviously, only be as good as its source. Good, reliable sources of information about terrorism and terrorists should be developed, and the information collected from them should be verified from other sources and processed so that it can be available in a useful form to those needing to use it for decision-making purposes. The information so gathered should be protected against the possibility of being filched by those affiliated with the terrorist cause. Those concerned with the provision of protective services should develop their own informal sources of information and should, in particular, cultivate persons with whom they can forge personal bonds of trust and on whom they can rely to obtain or receive information in times of crisis. *What is known in time can be avoided or frustrated.*

NOTES

1. This follows closely the recommendations made by the National Advisory Committee Task Force on Disorders and Terrorism. Contingency planning at all levels is heavily emphasized in each section of *Disorders and Terrorism*. The psychological aspects of this should not be overlooked. See the interesting article by Dalila Platero, "To Be Prepared Not to Be Prepared," 1 *Assets Protection*, No. 3, 1976, pp. 16-19.

2. It is as well to stress that there is really no such thing, from a security perspective, as an expert in terrorism. Certain persons have acquired special skills in the handling of the problems posed by terrorism through a specialized application of their own disciplines. Thus, a person having special skills in the area of threat assessment may have no special competence in the area of building security. Someone skilled in matters relating to bomb incident management might have little specialist experience to offer in the matter of kidnapping. When advice is sought, it is necessary to establish that there is proven competence in the particular matter on which guidance is required and that the necessary experience exists to authenticate the advice given.

3. See, for example, "Advising Negotiators on How to Deal with Terrorists," *Frontiers of Psychiatry*, May 1, 1977, p. 1. See, too, "Psyching out Terrorists," *Medical World News*, June 27, 1977, p. 15, especially "U.S. Experts: Psychiatrists Have No Magic," p. 16.

4. It must be assumed that determined, organized terrorist groups will use electronic surveillance devices even in the homes and other protected areas used by potential victims in order to obtain information on them. It is an important security task to conduct frequent searches for such equipment and to take appropriate measures in the event of discovery.

5. The victim is in much the same position, though worse, than one who is in a conventional prison system. This is indeed recognized in the language used by terrorists in

such situations, such as "people's prisons" and trial by "people's tribunals." The conventional prisoner is gravely handicapped without the ministrations of relatives and friends concerned, on the outside, with his well-being and interests; and he will need, too, the services of lawyers and others to free him from his predicament.

6. In view of the number of ruthless women terrorists now operating, it is pertinent to inquire whether those arming themselves in self-defense would be able to bring themselves to kill a woman in cold blood if the need arose. Those unable to employ weapons without squeamishness are safer leaving the task to others whose profession, training and inclinations more properly fit them for it.

7. This is especially important in the case of those kidnappings taking place in public and with great violence such as happened with both Schleyer and Moro. A rapid alert will allow specialist anti-terrorist forces to be mobilized to prevent the kidnappers leaving the area and reaching their prepared hideout. If they can escape the scene, the chances of apprehension and saving the victim are greatly diminished.

8. This is particularly so where the users are ordinary, non-technically trained persons. The greatest care should be exercised over code and passwords.

Conclusion

"...neither hardware nor security guards can overcome stupidity, carelessness or recklessness by the people using the building, and especially by those who may be the personal targets for attack. The degree of inconvenience and self-discipline to be tolerated must be balanced against the degree of risk to be accepted, but a manifestation of conscientious and disciplined protection is likely to be an effective deterrent in itself and will often induce the terrorist to transfer his attention to softer targets."

Richard Clutterbuck[1]

There is no substitute for prevention. The main thrust of this book, so far as it relates to the provision of protective services, is on meeting the threat *before* it materializes. Money and energy spent on heading off the enemy at the pass are an investment in future safety. Security *can* be bought at a price, and that price is never too high to pay. Spending a hundred thousand dollars on an executive training program may seem a luxury to a corporation that has not so far felt the biting fear of a terroristic campaign gnawing at its vitals. Once it has paid out a ransom of $5,000,000 to recover one of its executives, and the others have felt the chill hand of fear on their hearts, such a program may well seem exceedingly cheap at the price.

It has been stressed, too, that even this investment in preparing for the worst is no proof against terrorist attacks. It cannot be expected that even the most prolific expenditure of resources will provide infallible protection. But what is bought, if not peace of mind, is at least the knowledge that something practical and efficacious is being done about the problem. Perfect security is a utopian dream that no amount of money, no technological effort, in reality, can produce. Good security is that which is in the realms of practicality and is the product of expertise, investment, time, and effort. The result is a marked improvement over conditions that would otherwise obtain in its absence.

Good security is a necessary condition of governmental, commercial, industrial and personal efficiency where management is under attack by terrorists. Neither public nor private enterprises can function satisfactorily unless the necessary conditions of safety are guaranteed so far as is humanly possible. Terrorists are out to place an intolerable strain upon the system, a strain that would cause it to collapse in favor of the forces challenging it. The burden is clearly focused upon human beings both to suffer the challenge and to resist it. It is human beings who are assassinated, kidnapped, and taken hostage, and whose property is destroyed or taken from them. Resisting the terrorist and his evil designs is largely a matter of supplying people, the right people, with the will to resist and the knowledge of how to offer effective resistance. The provision of protective services is a necessary adjunct to the development of the spirit that will enable those against whom the terrorist attack is directed to provide the means for sustaining themselves against the shock of the blow and to turn back its force.

The human element in the provision of good security cannot be too strongly or repeatedly stressed. Human beings can make or break any system, however costly, and whatever the technical expertise that has gone into its design. Good security begins and ends with the human agent. Whatever the degree of technical sophistication reached, some element of human assistance will, somewhere along the line, be built into the system. This is our Achilles heel, the weak link in the strongest technical chain. Such an element, in the nature of things cannot be eliminated, and, in consequence, must be allowed for in the design of the system. If we have to accept the human element, as we must, the very least we can do is to see that it performs effectively to the best of its ability. The key words are *training* and *supervision.*

The acceptance of human fallibility and the knowledge that systems are breached through the errors of mere mortals ought not to be a source of resigned complacency or despair. There must be a constant striving for improvement for a reduction of the human error factor to the lowest possible margin. Improvement is possible, and the margin of human error can be reduced to within limits that are of comparatively little value to the antisocial forces against which the security barrier is erected. A head of the United States Secret Service has said,[2] "[There] is very little margin for error in our business. Therefore, we demand perfection." This search for perfection, even though it may be practically unattainable, is a most healthy exercise and a stimulus for a proper functioning of the security machine.

Those concerned with the provision of protective services must begin to look towards tomorrow's terrorism.[3] Tomorrow, indeed, will be upon us with frightening suddenness, and there is but little time left to prepare for its arrival. New weaponry, new tactics, new modalities, new levels of fearfulness must necessarily be faced by those to whose lot falls the response. As each new onslaught is thrown back, fewer and fewer options are left for terrorists. Those that remain are, perhaps, the most fearful that can be imagined, for it is their very awesomeness that has restrained their employment up to the present. As desperation works its way amid the terrorist ranks, the inhibitions on the use of these dread forces will grow weaker, and they will be unleashed upon society with frightening effect. It is essential that the proper preparations for their reception be made *now* in order that we are not taken by surprise and overwhelmed.

In its psychology and objectives, the new terrorism will not be so very different from the old. The human beings who will be behind tomorrow's terrorism will be very like those behind today's or yesterday's terrorism. It is as well, therefore, to study who they are, what they want and why they behave in this way. What they do to attain their objectives, how they do it, and the means they will employ, will be the creatures of their own time. Only the human element remains constant, and the lessons of history on how to cope with it must be thoroughly learned. Tomorrow's terrorism may well be very different from that which plagues the world today, and it will most certainly be difficult to imagine all its ramifications with the aid of contemporary terminology. It is safe to say, however, that tomorrow's terrorist, as a person, will not be so very different from those operating at the present time. For this reason, responses based on a sound knowledge of the human being behind the event are more likely to be effective than those seeking merely to speculate about the forms these frightful activities are likely to take in the future.

Some have suggested that, perhaps, terrorism is just a passing fancy and that too much attention is already being paid to it. Some, indeed, have felt, not without justification, that the attention paid to it by experts and laymen in our time has contributed in large measure to the magnification of the problem. Others, on the other hand, feel that terrorism is a growth industry, albeit an ugly one, and that inevitably the world is in for more of the same—only worse. This book subscribes, substantially, to the second school of thought, for, on the plain evidence, the possibilities are clear to see. Terrorism will remain for many the only form of political expression. For others, it will offer very real prospects of ascending to power as, already, it has assisted many in the past. It will continue to wax and wane in different societies and in different times as before. Some tactics will be improved, while others will pass out of vogue. Terrorism is a perpetual expression of Man's inhumanity to Man. For that reason alone, it may be regarded as being here to stay. All that can be attempted—and this book represents a modest contribution in that direction—is to try to keep it within manageable proportions.

NOTES
1. *Living With Terrorism* (New York: Alrington House Publishers, 1975), p. 64.
2. H. Stuart Knight, People, March 22, 1976, p. 59.
3. On this, generally, see Robert H. Kupperman, *Facing Tomorrow's Terrorist Incident Today* (Washington, D.C.: Law Enforcement Assistance Administration, 1977).

Bibliography

Aaron, Harold R. "The Anatomy of Guerrilla Terror." *Infantry,* vol. 58, March-April, 1967.

Abrahamsen, D. *Our Violent Society.* New York: Funk & Wagnell, 1970.

Adelson, Alan. *S.D.S.: A Profile.* New York: Scribner's, 1972.

Adkins, E.J., Jr. "Protection of American Industrial Dignitaries and Facilities Overseas." *Security Management,* vol. 18, no. 3, July, 1974.

"Aids to the Detection of Explosives—A Brief Review of Equipment for Searching Out Letter Bombs and Other Explosive Devices." *Security Gazette,* vol. 17, no. 2, February, 1975.

Alexander, Yonah, ed. *International Terrorism: National, Regional and Global Perspectives.* New York: Praeger, 1976.

Allback, D.M. "Countering Special-Threat Situations." *Military Police Law Enforcement Journal,* vol. 2, no. 2, Summer Quarterly, 1975.

Arendt, H. *On Violence.* New York: Harcourt, Brace, World, 1969.

Arey, James A. *The Sky Pirates.* New York: Scribner's, 1972.

"Atom Smasher at Stanford Hit by Two Bombs." *Los Angeles Herald Examiner,* December 8, 1971.

"Austria Seeks Atom Guerrilla." *Washington Post,* April 23, 1974.

Avery, Paul, and McLellan, Vin. *The Voices of Guns: The Definitive and Dramatic Story of the 22-month Career of the Symbionese Liberation Army.* New York: Putnam, 1976.

Barrett, R.J. "Indicators of Insurgency." *Military Review,* vol. 52, 1973.

Bassiouni, M. Cherif, ed. *International Terrorism and Political Crimes.* Springfield, Ill.: Charles C. Thomas, 1975.

Baumann, C.E. *The Diplomatic Kidnappings: A Revolutionary Tactic of Urban Terrorism.* Hague: Martinus Nijhoff, 1973.

Bayo, Alberto. *One Hundred Fifty Questions For A Guerrilla.* Translated by R.I. Madigan and Angel de Lumus Medina. Montgomery, Ala.: Air University, n.d.

Bell, J. Bowyer. "The Gun in Europe." *New Republic,* November 22, 1975.

Bell, J. Bowyer. *The Myth of the Guerrilla: Revolutionary Theory and Malpractice.* New York: Knopf, 1971.

Bell, J. Bowyer. *The Profile of a Terrorist.* New York: Columbia Institute of War and Peace Studies, n.d.

Bell, J. Bowyer. *The Secret Army: A History of the IRA.* London: Sphere Books, 1974.

Bell, J. Bowyer. *Transnational Terror.* Washington, D.C.: American Enterprise Institute for Public Policy Research, 1975.

Bennett, R.K. "Brotherhood of the Bomb." *Reader's Digest,* December, 1970.

Berkman, A. *Prison Memoirs of an Anarchist.* New York: Schocken, 1970.

Berkowitz, L., ed. *Roots of Aggression: A Re-Examination of the Frustration-Aggression Hypothesis.* New York: Random House, 1971.

Bern, Major H. von Dach. *Total Resistance.* Boulder, Colorado: Panther, 1965.

Berry, Clifton F., Jr. "Crime May Not Pay, But Terrorism Has—So Far." *Armed Forces Journal,* vol. 113, August, 1976.

"Bomb Attacks on French Nuclear Station Site." *London Times,* May 4, 1975.

"Bombs Damage Stanford Atomic Research Unit." *Los Angeles Times,* December 8, 1971.

"Bombs Hit Nuclear Site in France." *Washington Post,* May 4, 1975.

Bond, Thomas C. "Fragging: S Study." *Army,* vol. 27, April, 1977.

Bond, Thomas C. "The Why of Fragging." *American Journal of Psychiatry,* vol. 133, 1976.

Boulton, David. *The Making of Tania Hearst.* London: New English Library, 1975.

Bowden, Tom. "The IRA (Irish Republican Army) and the Changing Tactics of Terrorism." *Political Quarterly,* vol. 47, October-/December, 1976.

"British Hijack Spurs Criticism of Random Security Searches." *Aviation Week,* January 13, 1975.

Brodie, T.G. *Bombs and Bombing: A Handbook to Detection, Disposal and Investigation for Police and Fire Departments.* Springfield, Ill.: Charles C. Thomas, 1972.

Burnham, David. "Nuclear Agency Is Reported Ready to Oppose Special Force to Combat Terrorist Attacks at Facilities." *New York Times,* January 12, 1976.

Burton, Anthony M. *Urban Terrorism.* New York: Macmillan, 1975; Free Press, 1976.

Callanan, Edward F. "Terror in Venezuela." *Military Review,* vol. 49, February, 1969.

Carlton, David and Schaerf, Carlo, eds. *International Terrorism and World Security.* New York: Wiley, 1975.

Carnegie-Mellon University Transportation Research Institute. *Security of Patrons on Urban Public Transportation System.* Pittsburgh, Pa.: CMU-TRI, n.d.

Carr, Gordon, *The Angry Brigade: The Cause and the Case—A History of Britain's First Urban Guerrilla Group.* London: Gollancz, 1975.

Chambard, Claude. *The Maquis: A History of the French Resistance Movement.* Indianapolis: Bobbs-Merrill, 1976.

Clutterbuck, Richard. "Kidnapping." *Army Quarterly,* vol. 104, October, 1974.

Clutterbuck, Richard. *Living with Terrorism.* New York: Arlington House, 1976.

Clutterbuck, Richard. *Protest and the Urban Guerrilla.* London: Abelard-Schuman, 1973.

Clutterbuck, Richard. "Two Typical Guerrilla Movements: The Irish Republican Army and the Tupamaros." *Canadian Defense Quarterly,* vol. 1, 1972.

Clyne, P. *Anatomy of Skyjacking.* New York: Transatlantic Arts, 1974.

Codo, E.M. "The Urban Guerrilla." *Military Review,* vol. 51, 1971.

Cohen, G. *Woman of Violence: Memoirs of a Young Terrorist (1930-1948).* New York: Stanford University Press, 1966.

Conrad, Thomas R. "Coercion, Assassination, Conspiracy: Pejorative Political Language." *Polity,* vol. 6, 1974.

Conquest, Robert. *The Great Terror: Stalin's Purge of the Thirties.* New York: Macmillan, 1973.

Coogan, Tim Patrick. *The I.R.A.* New York: Praeger, 1970.

Cooper, H.H.A. "Terrorism and the Intelligence Function." *Chitty's Law Journal,* vol. 73, March, 1976.

Cooper, H.H.A. "Terrorism and the Media." *Chitty's Law Journal,* vol. 73, September, 1976.

Cooper, H.H.A. "The Terrorist and The Victim." *Victimology,* vol. 1, no. 2, June, 1976.

Craig, A. "Urban Guerrillas in Latin America." *Survey,* vol. 7, 1971.

Crotty, William J. *Assassination and the Political Order.* New York: Harper & Row, 1971.

Crozier, Brian. "Anatomy of Terrorism." *Nation,* vol. 188, 1959.

Crozier, Brian. *The Rebels: A Study of Post-War Insurrections.* London: Chatto & Windus, 1960.

Crozier, Brian. "Transnational Terrorism." *Annual of Power and Conflict,* vol. 1972-73, 1973.

Crozier, Brian. *Ulster: Politics and Terrorism.* London: Institute for the Study of Conflict, 1973.

Davies, Donald M. "Terrorism: Motives and Means." *Foreign Service Journal,* September, 1962.

Demaris, O. *America the Violent.* Baltimore: Penguin Books, 1970.

Demaris, O. *Brothers in Blood: The International Terrorist Network.* New York: Scribner, 1977.

Dillon, Martin, and Lehane, Denis. *Political Murder in Northern Ireland.* Baltimore: Penguin, 1974.

Dobson, Christopher. *Black September: Its Short, Violent History.* New York: Macmillan, 1974.

Dortzbach, Karl, and Dortzbach, Deborah. *Kidnapped.* New York: Harper & Row, 1975.

"Drama on the Desert." *Time,* September 21, 1970.

Drennon, William W. "Security: A 24-Hour, Seven-Days-A-Week Affair." *Journal of Property Management,* vol. 38, no. 3, May-/June, 1973.

Duff, Ernest A., and McCamant, John F. *Violence and Repression in Latin America: A Quantitative and Historical Analysis.* New York: Free Press, 1976.

Eggers, William. *Terrorism: The Slaughter of Innocents.* Chatsworth, Calif.: Major Books, 1975.

"El Al Stresses Terrorist Security, Advises Other Airlines Tel Aviv." *Aviation Week,* September 13, 1971.

Elliott, John D. "Action and Reaction! West Germany and the Baader-Meinhof Guerrillas." *Strategic Review,* vol. 4, Winter, 1976.

Elliott, John D. "Transitions of Contemporary Terrorism." *Military Review,* vol. 57, May, 1977.

Ellis, Albert, and Gullo, John. *Murder and Assassination.* New York: Lyle Stuart, 1971.

Ellis, Desmond. *Violence in Prisons.* Ashland, Ma.: Lexington Books, 1975.

Esson, D.M.R. "The Secret Weapon—Terrorism." *Army Quarterly,* vol. 78, 1959.

Fairbairn, G. *Revolutionary Guerrilla Warfare—The Countryside Version.* Middlesex, England: Penguin, 1974.

Faleroni, Alberto S. "What is an Urban Guerrilla?" *Military Review,* vol. 47, 1969.

Fanon, Frantz. *Wretched of the Earth.* New York: Grove, 1965.

"F.B.I. Fears Rise of A-Threats." *Los Angeles Times,* January 4, 1975.

Fielding, Byron. "Safety and Security in Multiple Family Complexes." *Journal of Housing,* no. 6, 1971.

"Fire at the AEC Plant Halts Warhead Production." *New York Times, June 25, 1969.*

Foxley-Norris, Chrostopher. "Entebbe and After." *Army Quarterly,* vol. 106, October, 1976.

Frank, Forrest R., "Nuclear Terrorism and the Escalation of International Conflict." *Naval War College Review,* vol. 29, Fall, 1976.

Frank, Gerold. *The Deed.* New York: Simon & Schuster, 1963.

Frank, Gerold. "The Moyne Case: A Tragic History." *Commentary,* December, 1945.

Fromkin, David. "Strategy of Terrorism." *Foreign Affairs,* vol. 53, 1975.

Fromm, Erich. *Anatomy of Human Destructiveness.* Greenwich: Fawcett World, 1975.

Gage, Nicholas. *The Mafia Is Not an Equal Opportunity Employer.* New York: McGraw, 1971.

Gann, Lewis H. *Guerillas in History.* Stanford: Hoover Institute, 1971.

Gaucher, Roland. *The Terrorists: From Tsarist Russia to the O.S.A.* Translated by P. Spurlin. London: Secker & Warburg, 1968.

Gellner, J. *Bayonets in the Streets: Urban Guerilla at Home and Abroad.* Ontario: Collier-Macmillan Canada, 1974.

Gerassi, F., ed. *Venceremos: The Speeches and Writings of Che Guevera.* New York: Simon & Schuster.

Gilio, M.E. *The Tupamaro Guerillas: The Structure and Strategy of the Urban Guerilla Movement.* New York: Saturday Review, 1972.

Gorney, Cynthia. "Twenty-Five A-Plant Safety Reports Sought After $50 Million Fire." *Washington Post,* August 14, 1975.

Gott, Richard. *Guerilla Movements in Latin America.* London: Thomas Nelson, 1970.

Green, Gion, and Farber, Raymond C. *Introduction to Security.* Los Angeles: Security World Publishing Company, 1975.

Greene, T.N., ed. *The Guerilla: And How to Fight Him.* New York: Praeger, 1962.

Greene, W., and Cockburn, A. "Case of the Paranoid Hijacker." *Esquire,* July, 1975.

Greene, Wase. "The Militants Who Play with Dynamite." *New York Times Magazine,* October 25, 1970.

Grivas, G. *Guerilla Warfare and E.O.K.A.'s Struggle.* London: Longman's, 1964.

Grodsky, M. "Protection of Dignitaries." *International Police Academy Review,* vol. 6, no. 4, October 4, 1972.

Guevara, Ernesto. *Guerilla Warfare.* New York: Random, 1961.

Guillen, Abraham. *Philosophy of the Urban Guerilla: The Revolutionary Writings of Abraham Guillen.* Translated by D.C. Hodges. New York: Morrow, 1973.

Hacker, Frederick. *Crusaders, Criminals, Crazies: Terror and Terrorism In Our Time.* New York: W.W. Norton, 1976.

Halperin, Ernst. *Terrorism in Latin America.* Beverly Hills, Calif.: Sage Publications, 1976.

Hamer, John. "Protection of Diplomats." *Editorial Research Reports,* VII, October 3, 1973.

Hannay, William A. "International Terrorism: The Need for a Fresh Perspective." *The International Lawyer,* vol. 8, 1974.

Hobsbawm, E.J. *Revolutionaries.* New York: New American Library, 1973.

Hoffacker, Lewis. "The U.S. Government Response to Terrorism: A Global Approach." *Department of State Bulletin,* March 18, 1974.

Hofstadter, Richard, and Wallace, Michael, eds. *American Violence: A Documentary History.* New York: Knopf, 1970.

Horowitz, Irving L., ed. "Political Terrorism and State Power." *Journal of Political and Military Sociology,* vol. 1, Spring, 1973.

"The Hostage: A Game of Terror." *Newsweek,* February 25, 1974.

Hubbard, David G. *The Skyjacker.* New York: Collier, 1971.

"Hunt Clue in A-Lab Bombing." *San Francisco Examiner, December 8, 1971.*

Huron, B.S. *Elements of Arson Investigation.* New York: Reuben H. Donnelly, 1963.

Hutchinson, M. Crenshaw. "The Concept of Revolutionary Terrorism." *Journal of Conflict Resolution,* vol. 16, 1972.

Hyams, Edward. *Terrorists and Terrorism.* New York: St. Martins's, 1974.

"Industrial Sabotage in Nuclear Power Plants," *Nuclear Safety,* vol. 2, March, April, 1970.

Ingram, Timothy H. "Nuclear Hijacking: Now Within the Grasp of Any Bright Lunatic." *Washington Monthly,* January, 1973.

International Business Machines Corporation. Data Processing

Division. *The Considerations of Data Security in a Computer Environment.* White Plains, N.Y.: IBM, July, 1970.

Jacks, Oliver. *Assassination Day.* New York: Stein and Day, 1976.

Jackson, Sir Geoffrey. *Surviving the Long Night: An Autobiographical Account of a Political Kidnapping.* New York: Vanguard, 1974.

James, T. "Rescuing Hostages: A *Time* Essay." *Time,* September 18, 1972.

Jenkins, Brian Michael. *The Five Stages of Urban Guerilla Warfare.* Santa Monica, Calif.: Rand, 1971.

Jenkins, Brian Michael. *International Terrorism: A New Mode of Conflict.* Los Angeles: Crescent Publications, 1975.

Jenkins, Brian Michael. *Soldiers Versus Gunmen: The Challenge of Urban Guerilla Warfare. Santa Monica, Calif.: Rand, 1974.*

Jenkins, Brian Michael. Terrorism and Kidnapping. Santa Monica, Calif.: Rand Corp., 1974.

Jenkins, Brian Michael, and Johnson, J. *International Terrorism—A Chronology, 197668-1974.* Santa Monica, Calif.: Rand Corp., 1975.

Johnson, D.F. "Guatemala—From Terrorism to Terror." *Conflict Studios,* no. 23, May, 1972.

Joll, James. *The Anarchists.* New York: Grossett & Dunlap, 1964.

Juillard, Patrick. "Les Enlevements de Diplomates." *Annuaire Francais de Droit International,* vol. 17. Paris: Centre National de la Recherche Scientifique, 1972.

Karagueuzian, Dikran. *Blow It Up! The Black Student Revolt at San Francisco State College and the Emergence of Dr. Hayakawa.* Boston: Gambit, 1971.

Karber, Phillip A.; Mengel, R. William; and Novotny, Eric J. "A Behavioral Analysis of the Terrorist Threat to Nuclear Installations." U.S. Atomic Energy Commission/Sandia Laboratories, July, 1974.

Karber, Phillip A., et al. *Draft Working Paper B., Analysis of the Terrorist Threat to the Commercial Nuclear Industry: Summary of Findings.* Vienna, Va.: The BDM Corporation, 1975.

Karber, Phillip A., et al. *Draft Working Paper C, Analysis of the Terrorist Threat to the Commercial Nuclear Industry: Supporting Appendices.* Vienna, Va.: The BDM Corporation, 1975.

Kelly, James. *The Genesis of Revolution.* Dublin: Kane, 1976.

Kelly, Joseph B. "Assassination in Wartime." *Military Law Review,* vol. 30, October, 1965.

Kennedy, T.L., and Johnston, G.W. "Civilian Bomb Injuries." *British Medical Journal,* vol. 1, 1975.

Kifner, John. "Toppler of A-Plant Tower Shocks New England Town With Protest." *New York Times,* March 2, 1974.

Kirk, P.L. *Fire Investigation.* New York: Wiley, 1969.

Kirkham, J.F., and Levy, S. *Assassination and Political Violence.* National Commission on the Causes and Prevention of Violence. Washington, D.C.: U.S. Government Printing Office, 1969.

Knopf. "Sniping Incident: A New Pattern of Violence." *Law and Order,* May, 1969.

Krieger, D.M. "Terrorists and Nuclear Technology." *Bulletin of the Atomic Scientists,* vol. 31, June, 1975.

Kurve, Mavin. "Mystery of Uranium Smuggling Deepens." *The Times of India,* May 7, 1974.

Laffin, John. *Fedayeen.* New York: Free Press, 1973.

Laqueur, Walter. *Guerilla: A Historical and Critical Study.* Boston: Little, Brown, 1976.

Laskey, Melvin J. "Ulrike Meinhoff and the Baader-Meinhof Gang." *Encounter.* June, 1975.

Leiden, Carl, and Schmitt, Karl M., eds. *The Politics of Violence: Revolution in the Modern World.* Englewood Cliffs, N.J.: Prentice-Hall, 1973.

Lenz, R.R. *Explosives and Bomb Disposal Guide.* Springfield, Ill.: Charles C. Thomas, 1976.

Lillich, R.B., and Paxman, J.M. "State Responsibility for Injuries to Aliens Occasioned by Terrorist Activities." *American university Law Review,* vol. 26, Winter, 1977.

Lineberry, William P., ed. *The Struggle Against Terrorism.* New York: H.W. Wilson, 1977.

Lipson, Milton. *On Guard: The Business of Private Security.* New York: Quadrangle, 1975.

"Living Dangerously in Berlin: Political Kidnapping of P. Lorenz." *Time,* March 10, 1975.

Lorenz, Konrad. *On Aggression.* New York: Bantam, 1970.

McFadden, Robert D. "Damage is Put in Millions in Blaze at Con Ed Plant." *New York Times,* November 14, 1974.

McGuire, Maria. *To Take Arms: A Year in the Provisional IRA.* London: Macmillan, 1973.

McKnight, G. *Mind of the Terrorist.* London: Michael Joseph, 1974.

McKnight, G. *The Terrorist Mind: Why They Hijack, Kidnap, Bomb and Kill.* Indianapolis, Ind.: Bobbs-Merrill, 1975.

McPhee, John. *The Curve of Binding Energy.* New York: Farra, Strauss & Giroux, 1974.

McWhinney, Edward, ed. *Aerial Piracy and International Law.* Dobbs Ferry, N.Y.: Oceana Publications, 1971.

Mallin, Jay, ed. *Terror and Urban Guerrillas: A Study of Tactics and Documents.* Coral Gables, Fla.: University of Miami Press, 1971.

Mangold, Tom. "The Case of Dr. Rose Dugdale." *Encounter,* February, 1975.

Marighella, Carlos. *For the Liberation of Brazil.* Harmondsworth: Penguin, 1972.

Marighella, Carlos. *Minimanual of the Urban Guerrilla.* Havana: Tricontinental, n.d.

Mickolus, Edward F. "Negotiating for Hostages: A Policy Dilemma." *Orbis,* vol. 19, Winter, 1976.

Morf, G. *Terror in Quebec: Case Studies of the F.L.Q.* Toronto: Clark Irwin, 1970.

Moss, Robert. "Urban Guerrillas in Uruguay." *Problems of Communism,* vol. 20, no. 5, 1971.

Moss, Robert. *Urban Guerrillas: The New Face of Political Violence.* London: M.T. Smith, 1972.

Moss, Robert. *The War for the Cities.* New York: Coward, McCann and Geoghegan, 1972.

Mullen, Robert K. *The International Clandestine Nuclear Threat.* Santa Barbara, Calif.: Mission Research Corporation, June 1975.

"Murder in the Sky: Easter Arilines, DC-9." *Newsweek,* March 30, 1970.

Najmuddin, D. "Kidnapping of Diplomatic Personnel." *The Police Chief,* vol. 40, no. 2, February, 1973.

Newman, Oscar. *Architectural Design for Crime Prevention.* U.S. Dept. of Justice. Law Enforcement Assistance Administration. Washington, D.C.: U.S. Government Printing Office, 1973.

Nieburg, H.L. *Political Violence: The Behavioral Process.* New York: St. Martin, 1960.

O'Mara, Richard. "New Terror in Latin America: Snatching the Diplomats." *Nation,* vol. 210, no. 17, 1970.

Paine, D. *Basic Principles of Industrial Security.* Madison, Wis.: Oak Security Publications, 1972.

Paine, Lauran. *The Assassins' World.* New York: Taplinger, 1975.

Parry, Albert. *Terrorism: From Robespierre to Arafat.* New York: Vanguard, 1976.

Paust, Jordan J. "Some Thoughts on 'Preliminary Thoughts' on Terrorism." *American Journal of International Law,* vol. 68, 1974.

Paust, Jordan J. "A Survey of Possible Legal Responses to International Terrorism: Prevention of Punishment and Cooperative

Action." *Georgia Journal of International and Comparative Law,* vol. 5, 1975.

Paust, Jordan J. "Terrorism and the International Law of War." *Military Law Review,* vol. 5, 1975.

Phillips, David. *Skyjack: The Story of Air Piracy.* London: Harrap, 1973.

Pike, E.A. *Protection Against Bombs and Incendiaries.* Springfield, Ill.: Charles C. Thomas, 1972.

Pierre, Andrew J. "The Politics of International Terrorism." *Orbis,* vol. 19, Winter, 1976.

Ponte, Lowell. "Better Do As We Say: This Is An Atom Bomb and We're Not Fooling." *Penthouse,* February, 1972.

Post, Richard S., and Kingsbury, Arthur A. *Security Administration: An Introduction.* Springfield, Ill.: Charles C. Thomas, 1970.

Powell, William. *The Anarchist Cookbook.* New York: Lyle Stuart, 1971.

Powers, Thomas. *Diana: The Making of a Terrorist.* Boston: Houghton Mifflin, 1971.

Rapoport, David C. *Assassination and Terrorism.* Toronto, Canadian Broadcasting System, 1971.

Robinson, Donald B. *The Dirty Wars.* New York: Delacorte, 1968.

Rose, Richard. *Northern Ireland: A Time of Choice.* Washington, D.C.: America Enterprise Institute for Public Policy Research, 1976.

Rosenbaum, David M. "Nuclear Terror." *International Security,* vol. 1, Winter, 1977.

Roucek, Joseph S. "Sociological Elements of A Theory of Terror and Violence." *American Journal of Economics and Sociology,* vol. 21, Spring, 1962.

Russell, Charles A., and Miller, Bowman H. "Profile of a Terrorist." *Military Review,* August, 1977.

Sale, Kirkpatrick. *SDS: Ten Years Toward a Revolution.* New York: Random House, 1973.

Schwarzenberger, Georg. "Terrorists, Hijackers, Guerilleros and Mercenaries." *Current Legal Problems,* vol. 24, 1971.

Segre, Dan, and Adler, J.H. "The Ecology of Terrorism." *Encounter,* vol. 40, 1973.

Shay, R. *The Silent War.* Salisbury: Galaxy Press, 1971.

Shellow, R., et al. *Improvement of Mass Transit Security in Chicago.* Pittsburgh, Pa.: Carnegie-Mellon University Transportation Research Institute, June, 1973.

Short, James F., Jr., and Wolfgang, Marvin E., eds. *Collective Violence.* Chicago: Aldine, 1972.

Shulman, Alix K. *Red Emma Speaks.* New York: Random House, 1972.

Silverman, Jerry M., and Jackson, Peter M. "Terror in Insurgency Warfare." *Military Review,* vol. 50, 1970.

Sinclair, Andrew. *Guevara.* London: William Collins and Sons, 1970.

Smith, Colin L. *Carlos: Portrait of a Terrorist.* New York: Holt, Rinehart, Winston, 1977.

Standing, P.D. *Guerrilla Leaders of the World.* London: Cassell, 1913.

Stechel, Ira. "Terrorist Kidnapping of Diplomatic Personnel." *Cornell International Law Journal,* vol. 5, 1972.

Steinhoff, Patricia. "Portrait of a Terrorist: An Interview with Kozo Okamoto." *Asian Survey,* vol. 16, September, 1976.

Stevenson, William. *Ninety Minutes at Entebbe.* New York: Bantam, 1976.

Stewart, Anthony T.Q. *The Ulster Crisis.* London: Faber, 1967.

Stewart, J., and Reid, R.R. *The FLQ: Seven Years of Terrorism.* Edited by F.B. Waler. Markham: Simon & Schuster, 1970.

Stoffel, Joseph. *Explosives and Homemade Bombs.* Springfield, Ill.: Charles C. Thomas, 1972.

Storr, Anthony. *Human Aggression.* New York: Atheneum, 1969.

Storr, Anthony. *Human Destructiveness.* New York: Basic Books, 1972.

Styles, S.G. "Bombs and Bomb Beaters." *International Defense Review,* vol. 9, October, 1976.

Styles, S.G. *Bombs Have No Pity.* London: William Lunscombe Publisher, 1975.

Styles, S.G. "The Car Bomb." *Journal of Forensic Science Society,* vol. 15, 1975.

Styles, S.G. "Defeating the Terrorist Bomber." *International Defense Review,* vol. 10, February, 1977.

Suchlicki, Jaime. *University Students and Revolution in Cuba, 1920-1968.* Coral Gables: University of Miami Press, 1969.

Sugg, Carolyn, ed. *Violence.* Paramus, N.J.: Paulist-Newman, 1970.

Symposium. "Skyjacking, Problems and Potential Solutions—A Symposium." *Villanova Law Review,* vol. 18, 1973.

"Task Force on Kidnapping." *External Affairs,* vol. 23, 1971.

Taylor, Telford, and Willrich, M. *Nuclear Theft: Risks and Safeguards.* New York: Ballinger, 1974.

Taylor, Telford. *Nuremberg and Vietnam: An American Tragedy.* New York: Quadrangle, 1970.

"Terror Through the Mails." *Economist.* September 23, 1972.

Tinnin, David, and Christensen, Dag. *The Hit Team.* Boston: Little, Brown and Co., 1976.

Toch, Hans. *Violent Men: An Inquiry Into the Psychology of Violence.* Chicago, Aldine, 1969.

Todd, Ian. *Ghosts of the Assassins.* New York: Seemann, 1976.

A Trust Betrayed, Namibia. New York: U.N. Office of Public Information, 1974.

Tuchman, Barbara W. *The Guns of August.* New York: Macmillan, 1962.

U.S. Congress. House of Representatives. Committee on Foreign Affairs. Subcommittee on the Near East and South Asia. *International Terrorism.* Washington, D.C.: U.S. Government Printing Office, 1974.

U.S. Congress. House of Representatives. Committee on Internal Security. *Political Kidnappings, 1968-1973.* Washington, D.C.: U.S. Government Printing Office, 1973.

U.S. Congress. House of Representatives. Committee on Internal Security. *Terrorism: A Staff Study.* Washington, D.C.: U.S. Government Printing Office, 1974.

U.S. Congress. House of Representatives. Committee on Interstate and Foreign Commerce. *Anti-Hijacking Act of 1973.* Washington, D.C.: U.S. Government Printing Office, 1974.

U.S. Congress. House of Representatives. Committee on Interstate and Foreign Commerce. *Anti-Hijacking Act of 1974.* Washington, D.C.: U.S. Government Printing Office, 1974.

U.S. Congress. Senate. Committee on the Judiciary. Subcommittee to Investigate the Administration of the Internal Security Act and Other Internal Security Laws. *Terrorist Activity.* Washington, D.C.: U.S. Government Printing Office, 1974.

U.S. Congress. Senate. Committee on the Judiciary. Subcommittee to Investigate the Administration of the Internal Security Act and Other Internal Security Laws. *Trotskyite Terrorist International.* Washington, D.C.: U.S. Government Printing Office, 1975.

Ursic, H.S. and Pagano, L.E. *Security Management Systems.* Springfield, Ill.: Charles C. Thomas, 1974.

Walter, Eugene Victor. *Terror and Resistance: A Study of Political Violence.* New York: Oxford University Press, 1972.

Walter, Eugene Victor. "Violence and the Process of Terror." *American Sociological Review,* vol. 29, 1964. p. 248.

Walzer, Michael. "The New Terrorists." *New Republic,* August 30, 1975.

Watson, Francis M. *Political Terrorism: The Threat and the Response.* Washington, D.C.: Robert B. Luce, 1976.

Watson, Frank M., Jr. *Political Terrorism: How to Combat It.* New York: McDay, 1976.

Wertham, F. *A Sign for Cain: An Exploration of Human Violence.* London: Robert Hale, 1968.

"When Tradition Comes to the Aid of Terrorism." *Economist,* March 17, 1973. p. 23.

Wilkinson, Paul. *Political Terrorism.* New York: Halsted Press, 1976.

Wilkinson, Paul. "Three Questions on Terrorism." *Government and Opposition,* vol. 8, no. 3, 1973. pp. 290-312.

Wilson, Jerry and Fuqua, Paul Q. *Terrorism: The Executive's Guide to Survival.* Houston, Gulf Publishing Co., 1978.

Witkin, Richard. "Hijacking Victims Returned as Cuba Holds 3 Suspects." *New York Times,* November 13, 1972. p. 1.

Wohlstetter, Roberta. "Kidnapping to Win Friends and Influence People." *Survey,* vol. 20, Autumn, 1974. pp. 1-39.

Wolfenstein, E.V. *Revolutionary Personality: Lenin, Trotsky, Ghandi.* Princeton: Princeton University Press, 1971.

Wolfgang, M.E., and Ferracuti, F. *Subculture of Violence: Towards an Integrated Theory in Criminology.* Scranton, Pa.: Barnes and Noble, 1967.

Woodruff, R.S. *Industrial Security Techniques.* New York: Doubleday, 1976.

Zartman, I. William, ed. *The Fifty Percent Solution: How to Bargain Successfully With Hijackers, Strikers, Bosses, Oil Magnates, Arabs, Russians, and Other Worthy Opponents in this Modern World.* Garden City, New York: Anchor Press, 1975.

INDEX

A

abduction 57
acceptable alternatives in hostage rescue operations 88
airport security 155
Anarchists 27, 149, 157
anti-assassination measures 42
anti-personnel bombings 102, 103
arson 93 (def)
assassination 25 (def)
assassination as a warning 28, 29
assassins, motivations 44, 45
Attica 141
avoidance 163, 167, 180

B

bacteriological warfare 102
bankrolling terrorist operations 119
bargaining situation 20
biographical dossier 176
blackmail 120
Blanco, Admiral Luis Carrero 26
bluff, fleeing felon 147
bodyguard 63
bomb technology 100, 101
bomb warnings 95
bombing 99
Bremer, Arthur 142
business 10

C

car bomb 97
Caransa, Maurits 69

careless talk   169
Cermak   27
chemical warfare   102
Chowchilla kidnapping   80
CIA   152
clandestine   19, 60
clandestine groups   4
collaboration   13
commitment to violence   139
communications   65, 75, 171, 178
conflicts of interest   70
confrontation style operations   137
contagion factor   42, 165
contamination   108
Connally, John   28
contingency planning   161, 162
"contract job"   30
coup d'etat   39
criminal kidnapper   62
crises management team   100, 177
cyanide compounds   102
cyclical factors   41

D

data, need for   18
debilitating effects   107
defective procedures   64
defensive driving techniques   67
denial   66
depersonalized   19
detection of explosives   101
division of labor   33, 60
dossier   176

E

economics of assassination   30
El Al   156

equipment 176
executive control of terrorist operations 129, 130
experience, need for in planning function 33
explosive device 99
extortion 59, 96, 119
    as a power play 122

F

false documentation 134
false sense of security 169
families 155
fast-breeder reactor 105
fear 3, 32, 139, 141
fire 93
fire bombing 93
flexibility in response to hostage taking 86
"foot soldiers" 129

G

Gaitskell, Hugh 51
gangs, professional 57
geographic analysis of trends 155, 156
glass, powdered 101
government involvement in hostage taking 80
"growth industry," terrorism as 178

H

Hanafi 140
hardware, need for right kind 40, 60
Hashshashin 26
hazardous behavior 4
Hearst, Patricia 59
Herrema, Tiede 72
hierarchical character of terrorist organization 128, 129
high-risk target 12

hostage taking   80 (def)
human element   177
human error   41, 177
human sentiment   18
human values   18

I

identification of terrorist groups   120
ideological target   45
imitative behavior   138
impersonal behavior   26
independent consultants   162
infiltration   4, 12
information gathering by terrorists   34
intelligence   35, 172
interests, interdependency   11
interests, tantible and intangible   8, 97
intimidation   8
Irish Republican Army   125, 136, 151
Israel   132
Italy   62, 159

J

Jackson, Geoffrey   67, 68
Japanese Red Army   126
Johnson, Lyndon   29
Jordan   84

K

Kennedy, John F.   28, 29
kidnap victim, moment of greatest danger   70
kidnapping   56 (def)
    means of gaining control of victim   57, 58
    overseas   70, 71

L

Latin American countries   10
Legionnaires Disease   105
local situations, need to study   181
Lod Airport   137
low profile in hostage situations   72, 73, 176
Lufthansa   156
Lumumba, Patrice   53

M

mail bomb   97
Malcolm X   44
martyr figures   120
mass communications   41
mentally disturbed individuals   136
mercenary relationship   30
micro-organisms   107
misfits   141
mock exercises   164
modus operandi   40
Mogadishu   84
motivation   43
M'Naughten   27
multiple hostage taking   83
Munich   83

N

national liberation movements   122
negotiation, public and private   82
"new" terrorism   177
nonconfrontation bombing   96
noxious substances   101, 102
nuclear weapons   98

O

Okamoto, Kozo   137
operatives   129
opportunistic attacks   37
opportunity as a factor in assassination   35
overcontrolled individuals   169

P

"palace revolts"   49
Palestinian liberation groups   125, 145
paranoia   32
Peel, Sir Robert   27
personal interaction in kidnapping cases   59
PFLP   84
planning   32, 33, 39
poisoning   101
poisonous gas   107
political kidnapping   62
political motivation as rationalization   137
political terrorists   20, 120
Ponto   132
prediction   29
preparation and planning   161
preventive measures   167, 176
private crisis team   82
procedural element of security systems   163
profile   119
"Propaganda of the Deed"   41
property interests   90
protection   3, 10
   private   10, 11
   public   10, 11
protective planning   32

protective services   1
  objective   5
  what   10, 17
  who   8
psychiatrists and psychologists   164
public figure   26
public purpose   26
publicity, avoidance of   73

Q

quasi-terrorists   17, 144

R

radioactive materials   105
ransom   70, 113
reduction of attacker's opportunities   39
rejection   3
reservoirs, vulnerability   106
resistance to change   65
response time   46
revenge   43, 142
risk assessment   9
risky behavior by individuals   170
Roosevelt, Franklin D.   28
roster of experts   164
routines   36

S

sabotage   92 (def)
  of transportation   92
safe havens in kidnapping cases   60
safe housing policy   170
Santucho, Roberto   131
Schleyer, Hanns-Martin   62

screening of contacts   12
security   3, 11
security analysis   20
security oversight committee   162
self-victimization   64
Sendic, Raul   131
sexual factors in terrorism   132
shield   80
siege mentality   178
skyjacking   83, 139
social reactions to kidnapping   56
Son of Sam   53
sophisticated security equipment   170
Southern Africa   123, 128
Spain   12
spectacular   29
stable target   36
Stockholm Syndrome   82
stress   31
subversive groups   4
suicide missions   133
supervision   177
surveillance   65
survey of security needs   162
survival techniques   59
survival training   59
Symbionese Liberation Army   121
symbolism   29

T

target hardening   65
target population   8
team concept   33
technology transfer   41
telephone communication in kidnapping   61
terrorism   3, 17 (def)
terrorist profile   119, 120, 134, 135
terroristic   3, 17
threat analysis   8, 35

threats, action to be taken 143
time, importance of 159
toxic substances 107
training 163, 177
transnational terrorism 124, 154 (def)
   with territorial ambition 126
   without territorial ambition 126
trends 151
Trotsky 13
Trujillo, Rafael 44
trust, need for 32
Tupamaros 113

U

Uruguay 113
utopian dream of perfect security 176

V

value dilemmas, property v. human life 90
victim resistance 66, 67
victim trauma 72
victimization 11, 153
victims, survival prospects 69
violent groups 4
vulnerability 156, 157

W

Wallace, George 142
weaponry 39, 40, 168
women assassins 43
women terrorists 132

X

Y

Yugoslavia, King Alexander of   51

Z

Zangara, Guiseppe   27

About the Authors

Richard W. Kobetz is an assistant director, Bureau of Operations and Research, International Association of Chiefs of Police. He directs research and projects in security and terrorism and conducts the IACP training programs on Protective Services, Hostage Rescue Operations and Crowd and Spectator Violence. He also has been an adjunct faculty member at the University of Maryland since 1973 and served as a member of the National Advisory Committee Task Force on Disorders and Terrorism.He brings to his present position law enforcement experience as a member of the Chicago Police Department. His publications include *Guidelines for Civil Disorders and Mobilization Planning, Criminal Justice Education Directory, Juvenile Justice Administration, The Police Role and Juvenile Delinquency, Crisis Intervention* and *The Police and Campus Unrest: Dialogue or Destruction.* Dr. Kobetz holds the associate degree in arts from City College of Chicago, a master of science degree in public administration from the Illinois Institute of Technology, the master of public administration and doctor of public administration degrees from Nova University.

H.H.A. Cooper is President of Nuevevidas International, Inc., a Texas corporation specializing in safety and survival techniques, and formerly Director, European and Middle Eastern Studies, Aberrant Behavior Center, Dallas, Texas. He was Staff Director, National Advisory Committee Task Force on Disorders and Terrorism. While serving as Director of the Criminal Law Education and Research Center of New York University, and Deputy Director of that University's Center of Forensic Psychiatry, he was special consultant to the National Wiretapping Commission and author of the Commission's comparative international report. He is presently a consultant on terrorism to the International Association of Chiefs of Police and various governmental agencies. A member of the Board of the International Society of Social Defense, he has represented that organization before the United Nations since 1972. Professor Cooper holds the bachelor of laws degree from the University of London, a master of arts in legal history from the University of Liverpool, and a master of law in criminal justice from New York University.